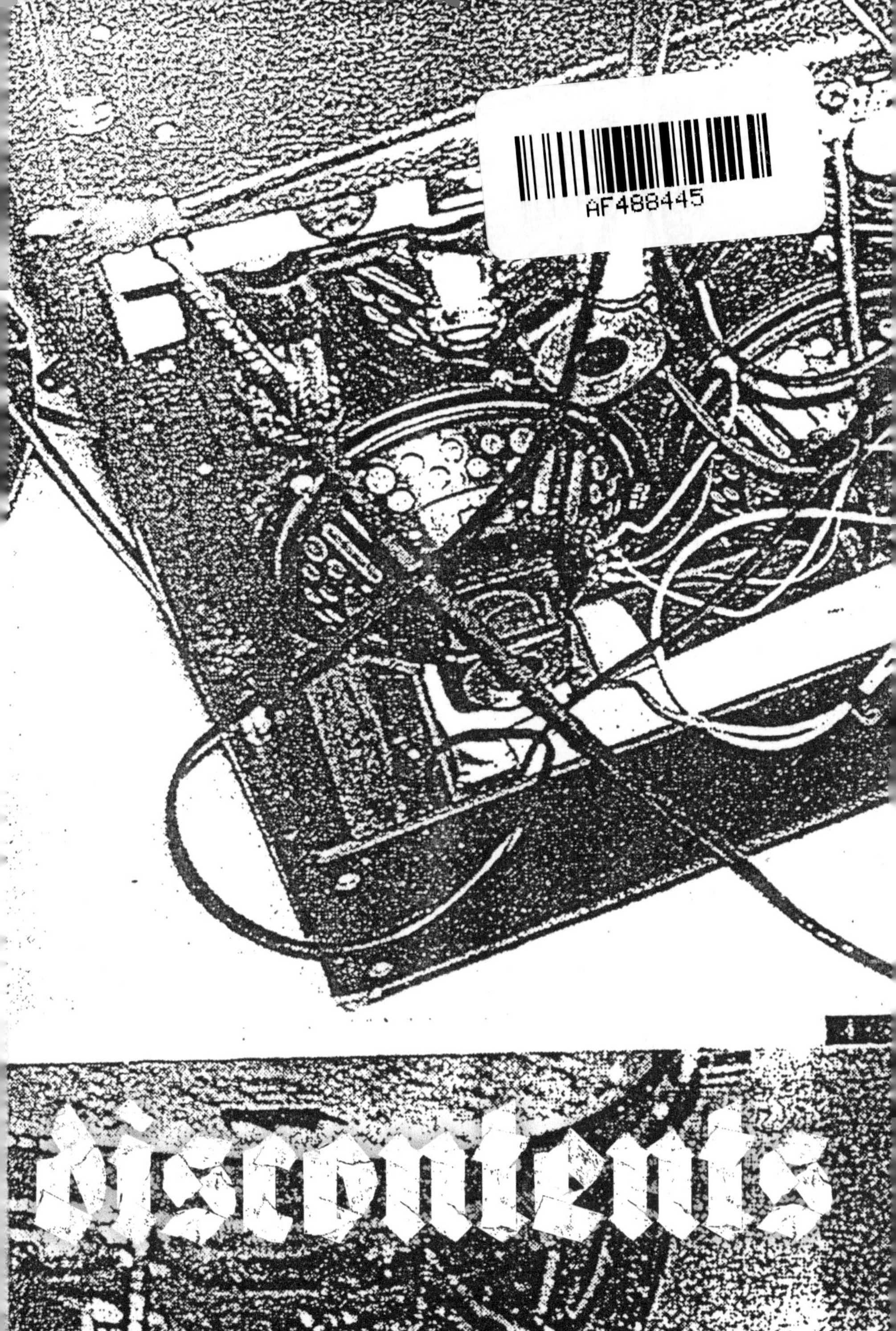
AF488445
Discontents

discontents

issue 1

EDITOR Roy Christopher
DESIGNERS Patrick Barber, Craig Gates
ARTISTS Tae Won Yu, Zak Sally, Marcellous Lovelace
PHOTOGRAPHERS Marnie Ellen Hertzler, Dave Young
WRITERS Cynthia Connolly, Timothy Baker, Andy Jenkins, Spike Jonze, Peter Relic, Greg Pratt, Fatboi Sharif

NAME DROPPING Claudia Dawson, Kristen Gallerneaux, John Mohr, Benjamin Tiven, Alap Momin, Erik Larson, Mike Manteca, Will Brooks, Andy Nelson, Marnie Ellen Hertzler, Alyssa Byrkit, Jim Byrkit, Dave Sardy, Jeffrey Alan Love, Natasha Stagg, Madeleine Byrne, Dave Tompkins, Mark Lewman, Nils Bernstein, David Grubbs, Kembrew McLeod, Joël Vacheron, Mark Slater, Erika M. Anderson, Rick Moody, Chad Foreman, Erik Ellington, Justin April, Boe Parries, Brian Ralph, Chicken Ramp Crew, and Lily Brewer: Thank you all.

ACKNOWLEDGEMENTS

Marcellous Lovelace's portrait of Fatboi Sharif was originally drawn for *Culture Power* 45.

Zak Sally's Unwound portraits were originally done for the Peel Session included in the Numero Group's final Unwound box set, *Empire*.

Spike Jonze's Michael Cooper piece is from the last, unreleased issue of *Dirt* magazine. Often referred to as "*Sassy* for boys," *Dirt* magazine was an early-1990s lifestyle magazine for teen dudes who were into music, videogames, and extreme sports. The publisher said the eighth issue was "too dark," but according to Andy Jenkins, the truth was that they'd given up on it already, much like the subject of Spike's essay. Spike once said, "Don't differentiate between 'This is a job' and 'This is what I'm doing for fun.' It's all simultaneous."

Andy Jenkins' "Drawing Lines" was originally in *Homeboy Magazine* #6.

Impeller Press books are published by Patrick Barber in Portland, Oregon, which was built on top of village sites of the Multnomah, Wasco, Cowlitz, Kathlamet, Clackamas, Chinook, Tualatin, Kalapuya, Molalla, and many other tribes who made their homes here. Today, members of these tribes and others are part of our community in the Portland metro area. We honor them with this land acknowledgement, and we give 5% of our gross sales to support Indigenous communities and the Landback movement. Please visit landback.org for more information on the Landback movement.

This book is printed to order, just for you. Thanks to this remarkable manufacturing technology, tiny publishers like myself are able to make books widely available without the cost or waste of excess books.

impellerpress.com

table of (dis)contents

columns

features

𝕰𝖉𝖎𝖙𝖔𝖗'𝖘 𝖓𝖔𝖙𝖊

**"There should be a science of discontent.
People need hard times and oppression to develop psychic muscles."**

—

from "Collected Sayings of Muad'Dib"
by the Princess Irulan in Frank Herbert's *Dune*

To be *discontent* is to be unsatisfied.

We don't see that as a negative ideation. We're not here to whine. We're here to win.

We're not nostalgic, but we'd be lying if there wasn't something alluring about turning real pages, exchanging real mail. The patina of packages sent and received, stamps licked and affixed, rubber-stamped and cancelled, address labels written and rewritten, the physicality of effort in every aspect.

We're not trying to recapture something from the past. We're trying to renew something else for the future. The idea is to bring back a sense of slow contemplation without losing the immediacy of the now. The breadth of time and the depth of attention.

This is the preface.

We all met when print was the vehicle for words and ideas, when paper was the hub of the social network. So, we made a zine together. Our interests are all here. Maybe some of yours are, too.

This is the pitch.

As for content, the watchwords were "cumulative culture." A lack of focus is a suicide pact, but we didn't want to define it until it existed. It's as serious as it is fun. We refuse to choose between being nerdy and getting our hands dirty.

This is the pilot.

We are unsatisfied. We are *discontents*.

Join us.

— ROY CHRISTOPHER, EDITOR

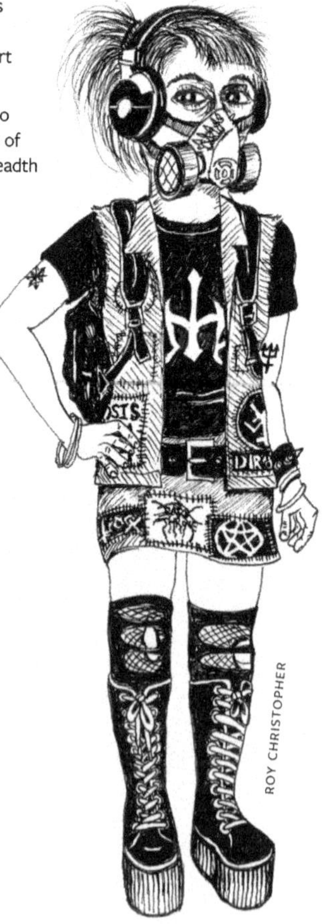

to the memory of

vern

rumsey

Charles Yu
Interior Chinatown: A Novel
Pantheon Books, 2020

Charles Yu's *Interior Chinatown* happens entirely in liminal spaces. It's all in the edges and on the edge. It's just as Manuel DeLanda writes in *A New Philosophy of Society* (2006): "In the case of ethnic communities, for instance, the enforcement of identity stories and categories occurs chiefly at the boundary" (p. 59). All of the doors in this story start out closed, and most of them never open. They are all quite visible.

Employing many of the conventions of screenwriting, Yu uses the discrimination of Hollywood casting to explore discrimination elsewhere. Roles like Generic Asian Guy, Old Asian Man, Dead Asian Guy, and the coveted King Fu Guy feel as

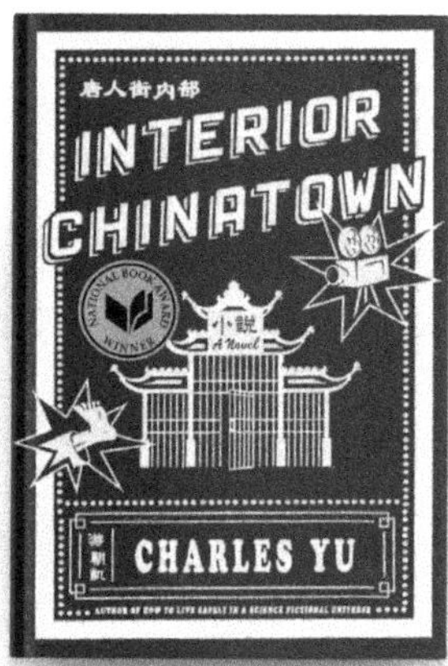

familiar as they do foreign, which is exactly the point. On the set of Black and White — so named both for its cop-show aesthetics as well as its racial designations (Black Dude Cop and White Lady Cop)—the Asian characters are all on the periphery. For *Interior Chinatown* however, those are the main characters. Bringing the edges to the middle further highlights the differences.

By turns heartbreaking and hilarious, poignant and important, *Interior Chinatown* further establishes Charles Yu as one our best cultural critics and commenters, as well as one of our best writers (see also his previous novel, *How to Live Safely in a Science Fictional Universe* [2011], and his short-story collection *Sorry Please Thank You* [2013], as well as his work on television [e.g., *Westworld*, *Legion*, etc.]). Here's to his continuing to open doors.

– Roy Christopher

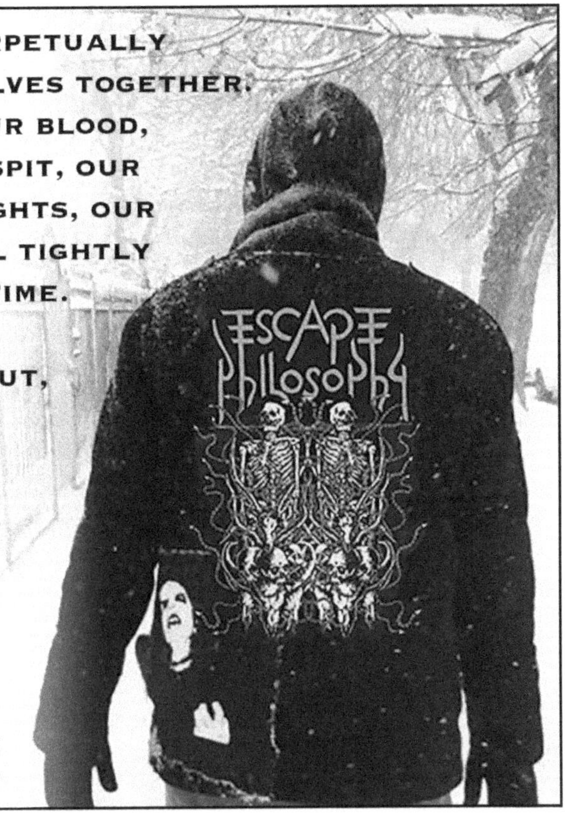

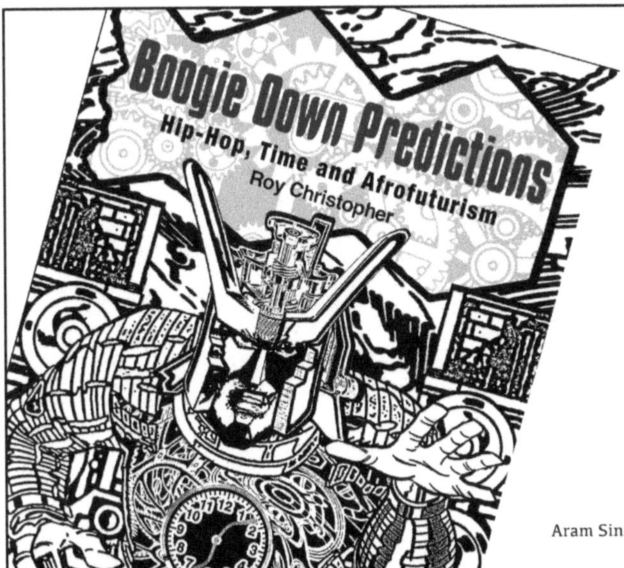

music ruined

I AM A FAILED RAPPER. There is no amount of sugar coating that will make my career seem anything more than that. A failure, a glorious, joyous, wonderful failure. You don't often find people who introduce themselves off the bat as a failure, but I figure why beat around the bush and pretend it is something it is not. There is no shame in failing, there is only shame in not trying, and if you know anything about me, I try to live as shame-free a life as humanly possible.

I am proud of my failure. My failure allowed me to do things that most people never get to do. I have been in every state in the lower 48, I have shared stages with the likes of Wu-Tang, Nas, Rage Against the Machine, MF Doom, Jay Electronica, etc. Shit, I even got to have a really awkward handshake moment with Public Enemy front-man Chuck D, who also introduced my group as we took the stage at the Bowery Ballroom. I have performed in Europe, played Red Rocks, and survived 5 years working solely as a musician. Yeah, I failed, but I had a pretty awesome time doing so.

I know this sounds like the sort of thing a failure would say to reconcile the pain of said failings, and ten years ago you would have been right, but now, I have enough distance between said failing and the current iteration of myself. When I look back at that asshole from ten years ago, I see a sad man-child filled with false bravado and alcohol as a way to numb the uncertainty that comes with failing and provides the courage to face the world.

I am happy to no longer be that person, the past ten years have allowed me to learn who I am, get myself physically and emotionally healthy, and move on with my life. While I may not like the person who initially came out on the other side of that journey, I can't help but be proud of the fact that the journey was taken.

I was fortunate enough to find myself in a strange brand of hip-hop based on the tenants of the art form mixed with the DIY punk ethic of the 1980s and breaking or at least trying to break the musical norms. I was able to take the work I put into the mid-'90s indie scene in NYC and carry that over into the mid and late 2000s as a full-time touring musician before I decided that I no longer could exist in that world if I hoped to ever exist at all. I had no desire to become the sad cautionary tale nor did I want to be the bitter old man who blames everyone and everything for his lack of success.

I knew from the start that the concept of success making music in the style that I made music looked wildly different than the idea of success tied to your Kanye West's and Jay-Zs. My hope was to make enough money to live a simple life and go as long as it was still fun, and even that was a long shot at best. If I was able to do this and maybe end up posthumously discovered and recognized in the future as an unheralded genius that would have been a best-case scenario. Having recently gone back and listened to my early work there is little-to-no chance of that happening. *to be continued . . .*

— **ti mothy**

my life

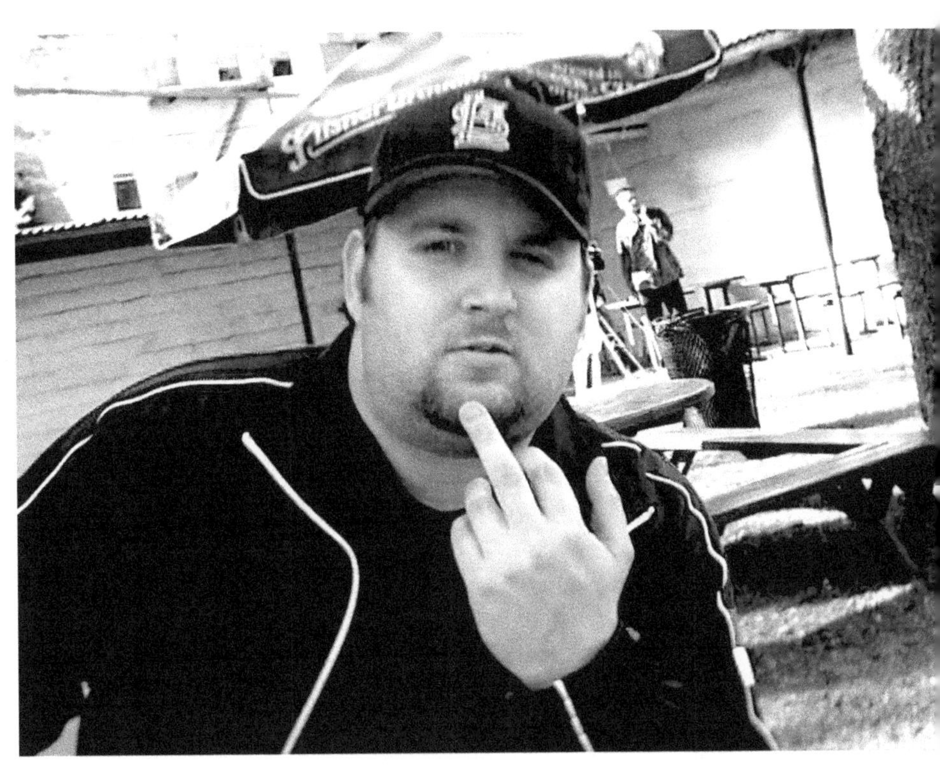

bake r

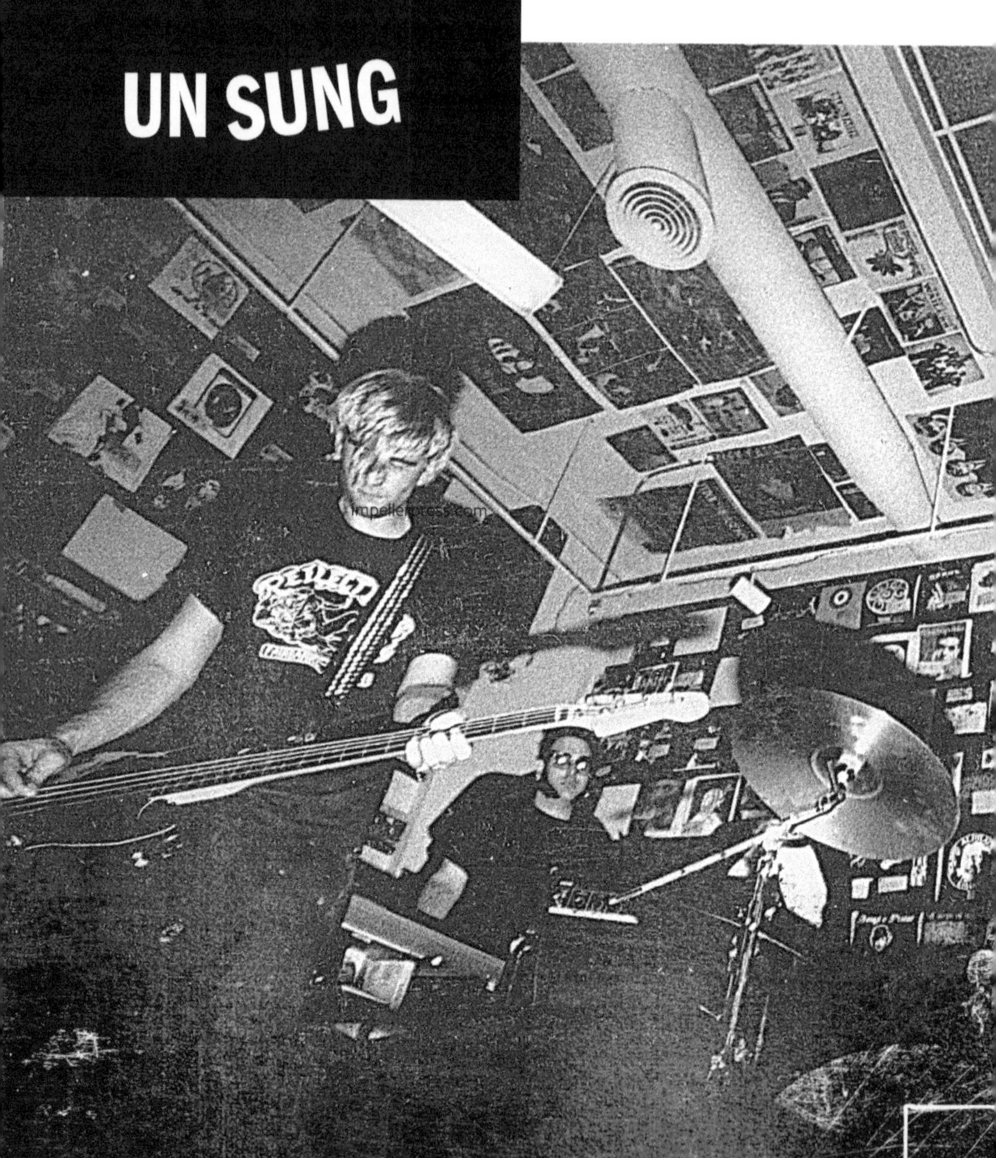

I often make a distinction between my favorite bands and the
bands I think are the best. Unwound is one of the few bands
for which that distinction means nothing: They are both one
of my all-time favorite bands and one of the best to ever do it.
Unwound have now been apart longer than they were together;
but every time I listen to one of their records, I am reminded
just how great they were.

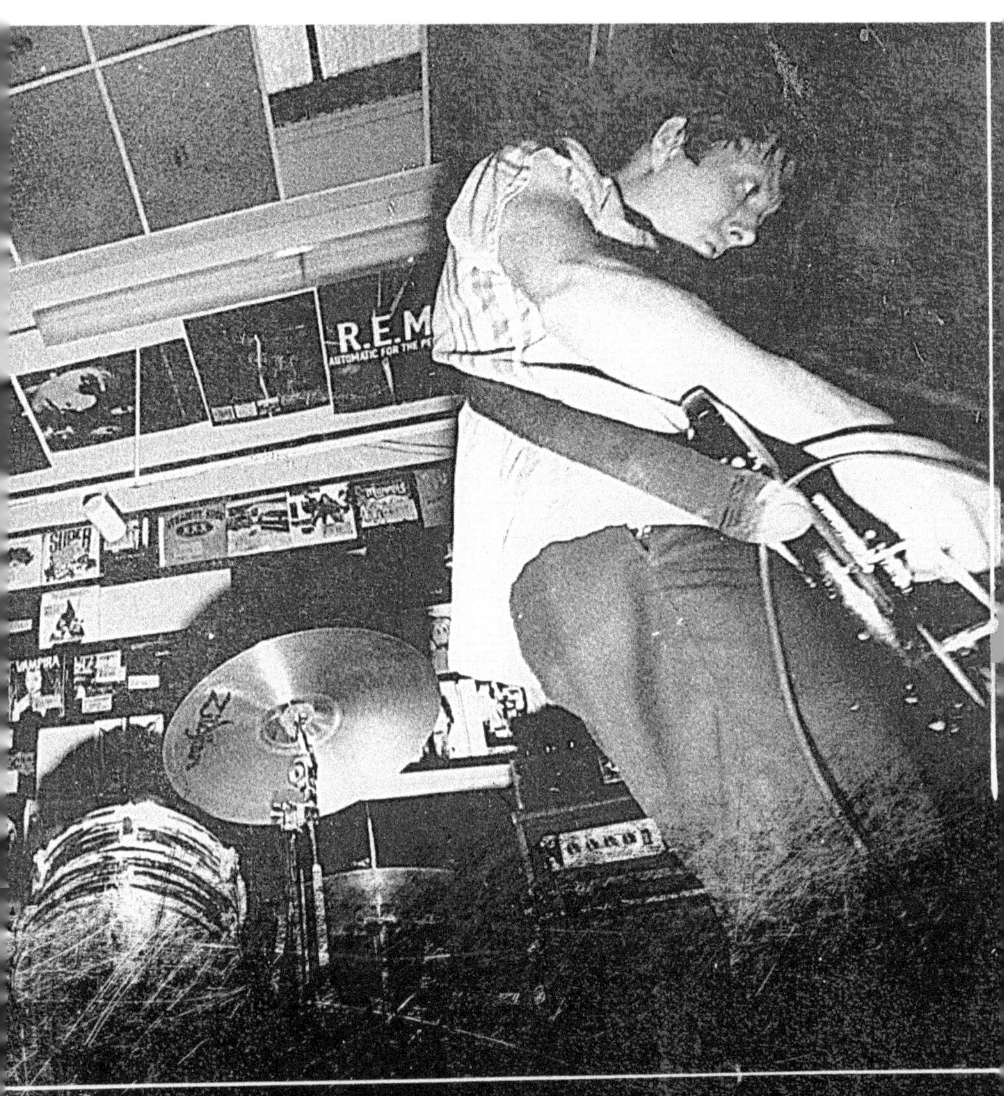

Having moved to the Pacific Northwest in the summer of 1993, I was trying to ease myself into the then-exploding local music scene. Their recent national attention had me already familiar with many bands and labels, but there were many more that only had fame and notoriety in their home region. I was digging deeper.

That's when I found Unwound

On a trip to Alaska that winter, I bought *Fake Train* (Kill Rock Stars, 1993). I still have vivid memories of falling asleep to it on headphones every night during that trip, immersed in basement darkness and new sounds. Some of my favorite songs still are from that initial exposure. I was hooked. I bought *New Plastic Ideas* (Kill Rock Stars, 1994) on vinyl at Mother Records in downtown Tacoma the day it came out.

In the book included in Numero Group's extensive Unwound boxset, *What Was Wound* (2016), David Wilcox writes that *The Future of What* (Kill Rock Stars, 1995) "would prove to be not so much a radical departure as the sound of a band growing restless, clinging to their past even as they lashed out against it…" (p. 131). Oddly, this is what all of their records sounded like to me, each at the time that it came out.

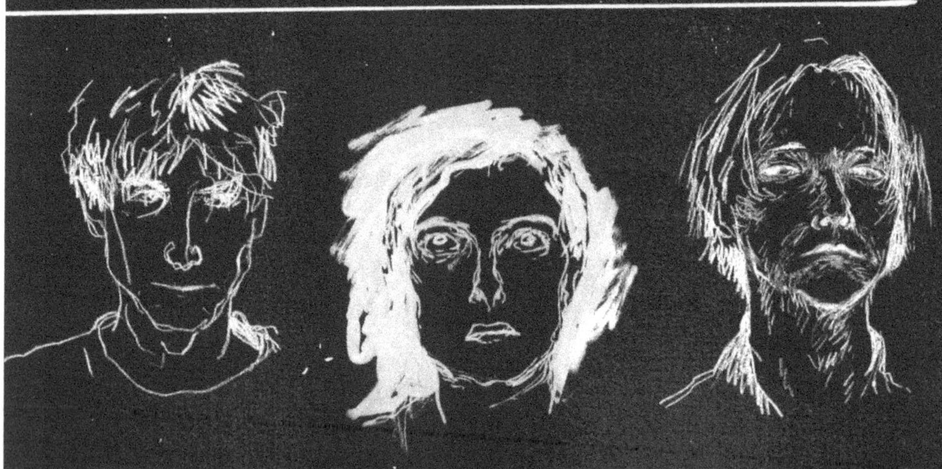

As Justin told me in 1998, "Well, sometimes you go into the studio with an idea, and you come out with something totally different… Every one of our records has its own purpose. I don't think we've aimed too high, and I don't think any of our records are perfect."

Unwound started out with a different drummer. Brandt Sandeno had been their drummer when he, Justin Trosper (guitar/vocals), and Vern Rumsey (bass) were called Giant Henry. Brandt moved on about the same time the band was moving on to something larger, more definitive. They recorded one record as Unwound, but it wouldn't be released until they'd become a sonic

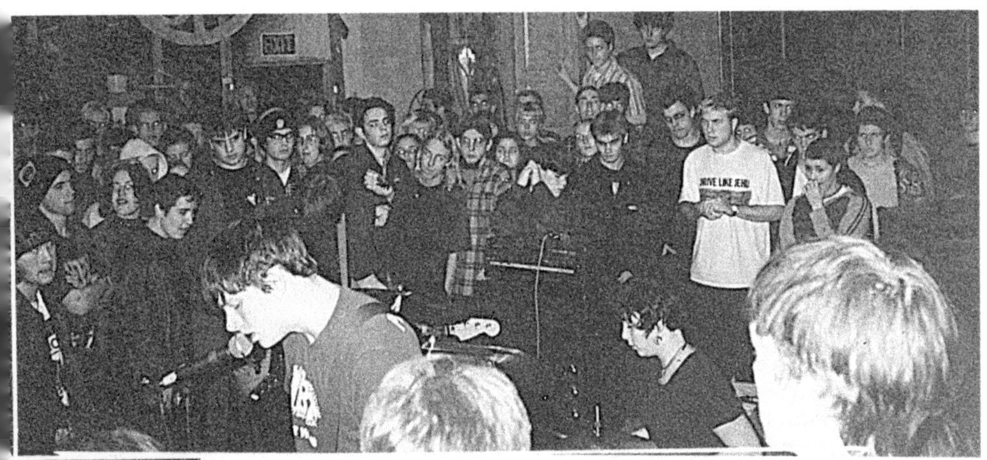

Lost in the Capitol Theater crowd, Olympia, WA, 1994. Photo by Roy Christopher

force beyond their 3-piece aspirations. Something special was emerging. The missing piece was Sara Lund.

Everyone involved — even Brandt — will admit that Unwound wasn't truly Unwound until Sara started playing drums. Like most great bands, the Justin/Vern/Sara line-up didn't waver until the three were no longer a band.

Numero Group's commemorative box includes 10 CDs, a DVD, and the aforementioned 256-page, hardback book. The DVD includes various live and candid clips of Unwound from throughout their 11-year lifespan, including footage from the one time I saw them play (pictured above): April 10, 1994 at the Capitol Theater in Olympia, Washington. Unwound was opening for Jawbreaker while the latter was touring their last good record, *24-Hour Revenge Therapy* (Tupelo/Communion, 1994).

These home movies from all phases of Unwound's existence illustrate not only their unsung greatness but also just how hard they worked at it. Unwound was one of the best bands to push sounds through speakers and commit those sounds to tape.

UNSUNG: A reconsideration of cultural forces and artifacts that didn't get their due in their time or that deserve a bump in light of recent developments.

Words: Roy Christopher   Layout: Craig Gates   Illustration: Zak Sally

1Q: with Fatboi Sharif

Q: *If Hip-hop didn't exist, would we have to invent it?*

A: being lost at sea searching home
analyzed ideas not yet seen
or harbored upon being proper
presentation made directions
involved as times later savagery
in its worst form at 1st celebrated
then vile transactions display
a eyes telescope back hallways
powerful paragraphs
rhymetic formats speak of power
needs for change infant next
world leaders womb expand
injected by hunger

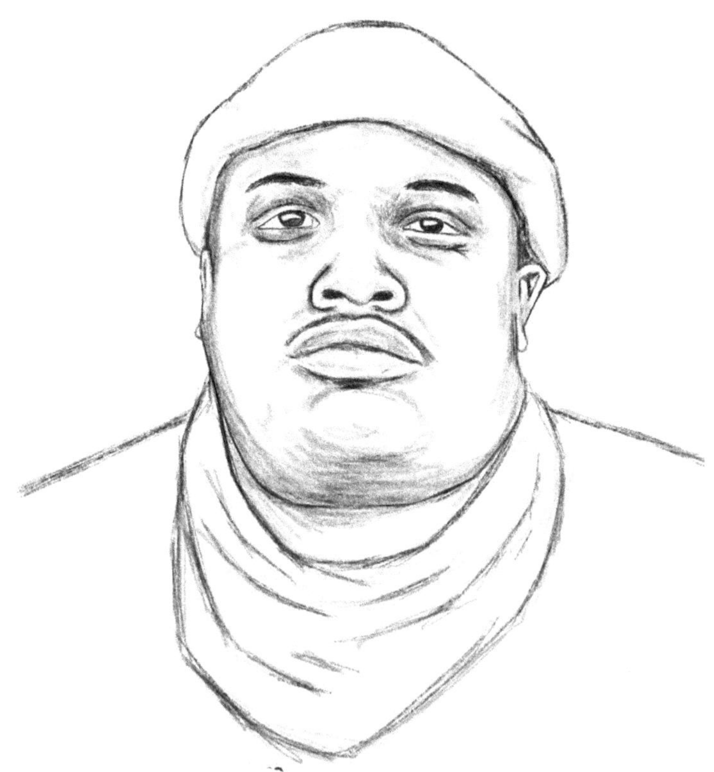

to deliver knowledge where
ink colored eyelids may retreat verbal
justice rose thru concrete
heaven amongst us purgatory
scripts non sanctioned
unveiling story
. . . i welcome hip-hop to the world

FATBOI SHARIF = lyricist, musician, artist, abstract creative vessel of power and elaborate literature. He was covered in The April 2021 issue of *The Wire* and the Spring 2021 issue of the *BB Document*, as well as *Complex*, *Spin*, and *Stereogum*. He tweets at @fatboyprospect. Check out his latest on Bandcamp: https://fatboisharif.bandcamp.com

One of the last songs that Ian Curtis wrote and recorded with Joy Division was called "Ceremony." They recorded it four days before he hanged himself. It was also the first song that New Order recorded and released after his death.

I don't know if the band is named after the song. I didn't ask. The threshold the song crosses is a convenient framing device for the talking about the band.

Some of my favorite records are the ones where a band leaps outside the bounds of their past and sets out for ground where their fans might not be willing to follow. I'm thinking of Cave In after *Until Your Heart Stops: Jupiter* polarized their existing fans, while *Antenna* proved they were onto something new; Corrosion of Conformity's definitively metal years, starting with *Blind,* but culminating in the Pepper Keenan-led *Deliverance* and *Wiseblood;* and even Kill Holiday's last record, *Somewhere Between the Wrong is Right,* on which they abandoned aggressive hardcore for an energized gothic-pop sound, by turns reminiscent of The Smiths, The Cure, and Ride.

> 66 **For the relatively well educated and financially secure, irony functions as a kind of credit card you never have to pay back.** 99
>
> – Christy Wampole, *The New York Times*

Ceremony has made such a transition on almost every release. Like their contemporaries in bands like Nothing and Cold Cave, the members of Ceremony moved from hardcore punk to expansive sounds from other genres. Just going back through their last three records will give you an idea: *Zoo* (Matador, 2012) is on the punk side of post-punk, *L-Shaped Man* (Matador, 2015) is the post part of post-punk, and *In the Spirit World Now* (Relapse, 2019) is something else entirely. To put it my previous terms, *In the Spirit World Now* is the New Order to *L-Shaped Man*'s Joy Division. To wit, the beginning drum pattern on "Further I Was" sounds a lot like the beginning of New Order's classic "Blue Monday." Even still, unlike other bands who get the spirit but lose the feeling, Ceremony is always on the way to something new.

"The only way to keep it interesting for us is to be creative and make new things," guitarist Andy Nelson tells me about their chronic transitions, "and so, it's never been conscious. It

MONY

conscious. It really is just the records that have come out have just been what happens when we get in a room to write." The five people in that room are Andy Nelson (guitars), Anthony Anzaldo (guitars), Justin Davis (bass), Jake Cassarotti (drums), and Ross Farrar (vocals). The constant push in new directions seems to be at least in part due their diet of art and media. "I think everyone in the band is such consumer of art and music and literature that we're inspired by making stuff. It would just be boring, and it's unsustainable for us to go make the same record five or six times in a row."

TURN AWAY AND TURN AGAIN THIS TIME

Broadly speaking, irony is the rhetorical strategy of saying one thing yet meaning another, usually the opposite. It also might be the most abused trope of our time. It has exceeded substance surpassing style and elevated into the absurd over the authentic. It's been a "get out of judgment free" card for as long as I can remember. In the preface to his 1999 book, For Common Things, Jedidiah Purdy frames the overbearing irony of our era as a defense mechanism: "It is a fear of betrayal, disappointment, and humiliation, and a suspicion that believing, hoping, or caring too much will open us up to these." It's an escape route, an exit strategy, a way off the hook in any situation, and it's become the dominant mode of pop culture. To live in the image of irony is to avoid risk. It means not ever having to mean. Purdy continues, "Irony is a way of refusing to rely on such treacherous things."

One way out is to risk those treacherous things, to stand firm on uncertain ground.

"That to me is an antidote to irony culture, because irony is a closed loop, a cage." Andy professes. "Ceremony's never been afra[id]   risk
... for exposing ourselves creatively

be_ause _ _ny is a closed loop, a cage," Andy professes. "Ceremony's never been afraid to risk ridicule for exposing ourselves creatively. When irony manifests itself as a band or something, it's a dead end. I read a lot of Mark Fisher's stuff, and I connected with a lot stuff like that, creatively."

Fisher was always looking for a way through the irony of our times. In *Ghosts of My Life* (ZerO Books, 2014), Fisher wrote of a scratchy cassette recording of Ian Curtis under hypnosis, picturing himself at 28, traveling through futures yet unseen. That ontological myopia, an insurmountable blindspot on the horizon, was a recurring theme in Fisher's writings.

"One of the through-lines of his observations about culture, both artistic and also in a general sense," Andy continues, "is people's inability to envision the future. It's funny because as both a member of Ceremony and other bands, I really connected with that as someone who always wants to make new things."

Ian Curtis never made it to 28. He died five years shy, and New Order said that they felt they had lost their eyes. I got an email from Mark Fisher just five days before he died. I'm still not sure how to feel about that.

> **66** **Places are leaky containers... What we call places are stable locations with unstable converging forces that cannot be delineated either by fences on the ground or by boundaries in the imagination—or by the perimeter of the map. 99**
>
> — Rebecca Solnit, *Infinite City: A San Francisco Atlas*

AVENUES ALL LINED WITH TREES

William Gibson once said that suburbs were more dangerous, because in the city they might steal your wallet, but in the suburbs they will steal your soul. Lying about 50 miles north of San Francisco, Rohnert Park, California is not exactly a suburb. As a planned community, the vibe is certainly suburban. It's known for its "family-friendly infrastructure." Its motto is "The Friendly City."

"It's exactly what you think," Andy says, "cul-de-sacs and identical looking houses. Each section is... If you live in the M section, all of the street names start with M. Like Ross used to live on Melody Drive, but Melody Drive intersected with another M street or whatever. And even if you look at the street signs, they look the same if you look at them quick. You can imagine how strange... and how that must seep into your persona or your psyche or whatever, and then put that into the abstract, in terms of thousands of people who live there. Also, the fact that in these planned communities, the subtext is, 'we're going to plan a perfect place to live.'"

"B_ _ _ _ _ised i_ _ _ suburbs was like being raised on a distant _d planet," wr_ _ s
vo_ _ _ _ _ _ _ _ _ _ _ _ _ _ _ _ _ _ _ *Society Verse* (F_ _ _ _ _ _ _ _ _ _ _ _ _ _ _ _ _at

the subtext ..., we're going to plan a p....

"Being raised in the suburbs was like being raised on a distant red planet," writes vocalist Ross Farrer in his book, *Society Verse* (Bridge Nine, 2010). "There is a cynicism that has been lodged into my subconscious, a black of mind and mouth that I've been trying to tear myself from."

After a stint in The City, Ross moved back to Rohnert Park. He writes, "I live here because I didn't want to live in San Francisco or Oakland anymore, because it was pitted in my soul that I belonged under a sky unblocked by lamplight, a place where I wasn't fused by constant chatter, noise from the urban onslaught. I learned that I actually love the place where I came from."

"Yeah, I think he really loves that whole area," Andy adds. "On our new record, there's this poem that runs through the whole thing. I think it's very literally about driving from San Francisco back up to Sonoma county, and the geography of that part of California is pretty central to the band throughout."

THEN AGAIN, THE SAME OLD STORY

Ceremony might not be named after the song, but it would make sense if they were. Bernard Sumner talks and writes about where he grew up much in the way that Ross Farrar does, with love and disdain all the same. As they say, you can't run from where you come from, even if you're only standing firm on uncertain ground.

After all, "Radio Head" is the name of a Talking Heads song.

WORDS: Roy Christopher
LAYOUT: Craig Gates

ST

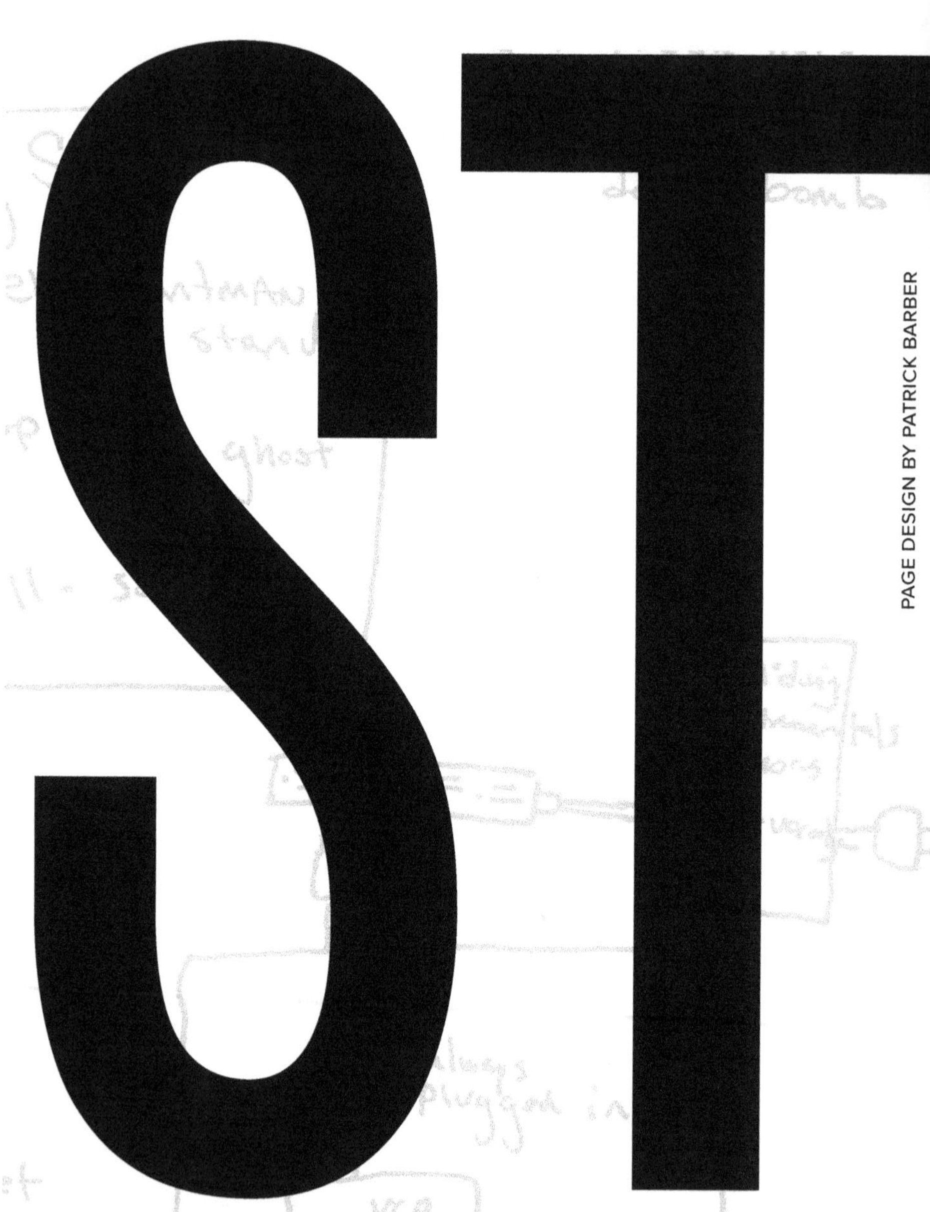

A Tribute to Hsi-Chang Lin
by Roy Christopher

Composer John Cage, who despised the idea of recorded music, once said, ". . . music instructs us, that the uses of things, if they are meaningful, are creative; therefore the only lively thing that will happen with a record, is, if somehow you could use it to make something which it isn't."[1]

Hsi-Chang Lin, also known as Still, was forever using records to make something else. Chang went so far as to use the turntable in ways I've never seen anyone before or since use it. He was truly taking the constraints of a system, bending them, and often breaking them to do what he wanted.

After Cage above, it has also been said that DJs play records and turntablists play turntables. Chang was doing whatever the next thing would be.

In one of the last of our many online chats, Chang and I dubbed his music *drone-hop*. His sound was noisy and ambient yet often abrasive, with brutal, banging beats. It wasn't industrial. It wasn't mechanical. It was a living hip-hop-noise organism, but one to be filed in a phylum all its own.

"Turntables are an *oral* instrument," he wrote in one of his notebooks

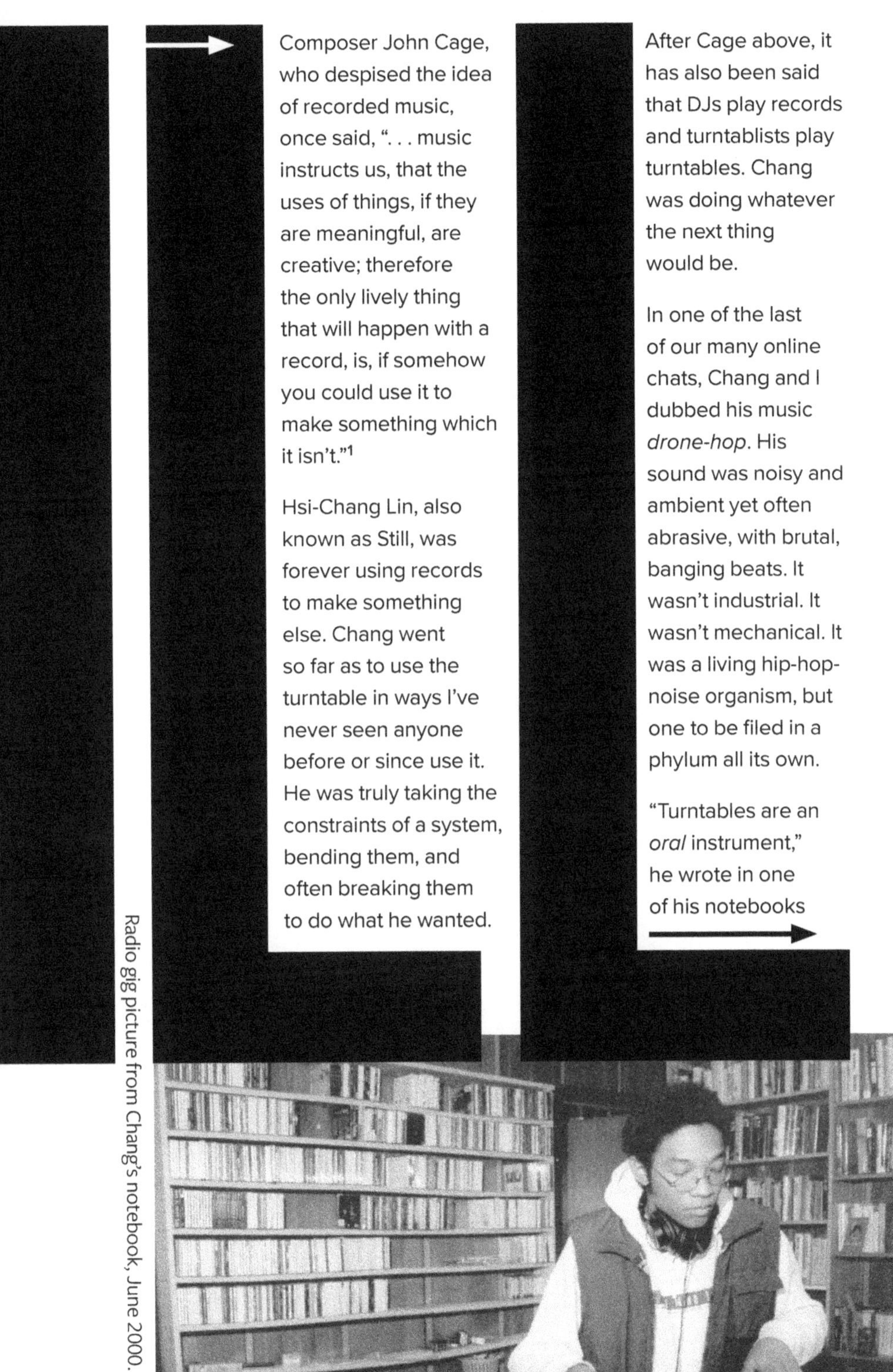

from 2000 (his emphasis), "based on *orality*!" This note echoes both Public Enemy ("Terminator X speaks with his hands!"[2]) and one of the founders of media ecology, Walter Ong ("Today, it appears, we live in a culture or in cultures very much drawn to openness and in particular to open-system models for conceptual representations. This openness can be connected with our new kind of orality, the secondary orality of our electronic age . . ."[3]). It's evident from these early notes that Chang was thinking hard about what the turntable could do and be, and that he was not only trying to create new sounds but also new spaces in which they could be experienced. His was a pure exploration in a spirit as much Laurie Anderson and Brian Eno as it was Christian Marclay and Grandmaster Flash.

Along with emcee Will Brooks and producer Alap Momin, Chang is probably best known as the DJ behind the group dälek. Alap told me the story of how Chang came to join them:

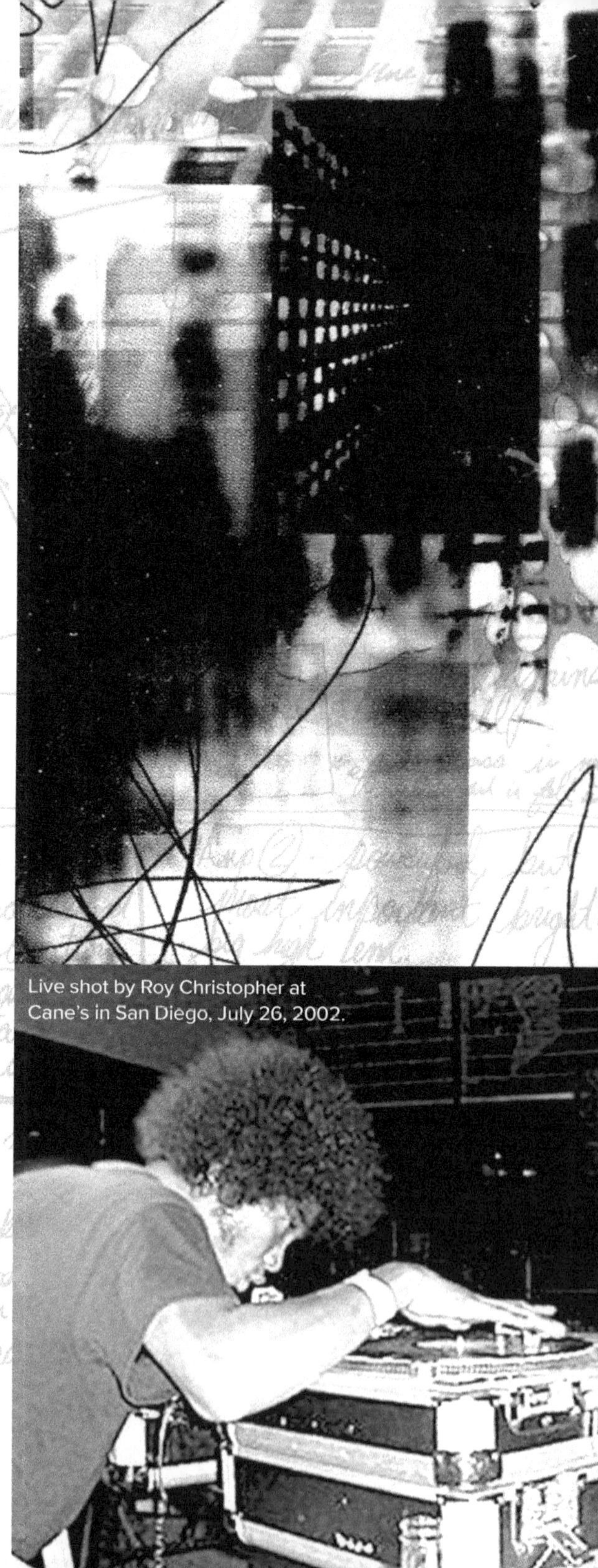

Live shot by Roy Christopher at Cane's in San Diego, July 26, 2002.

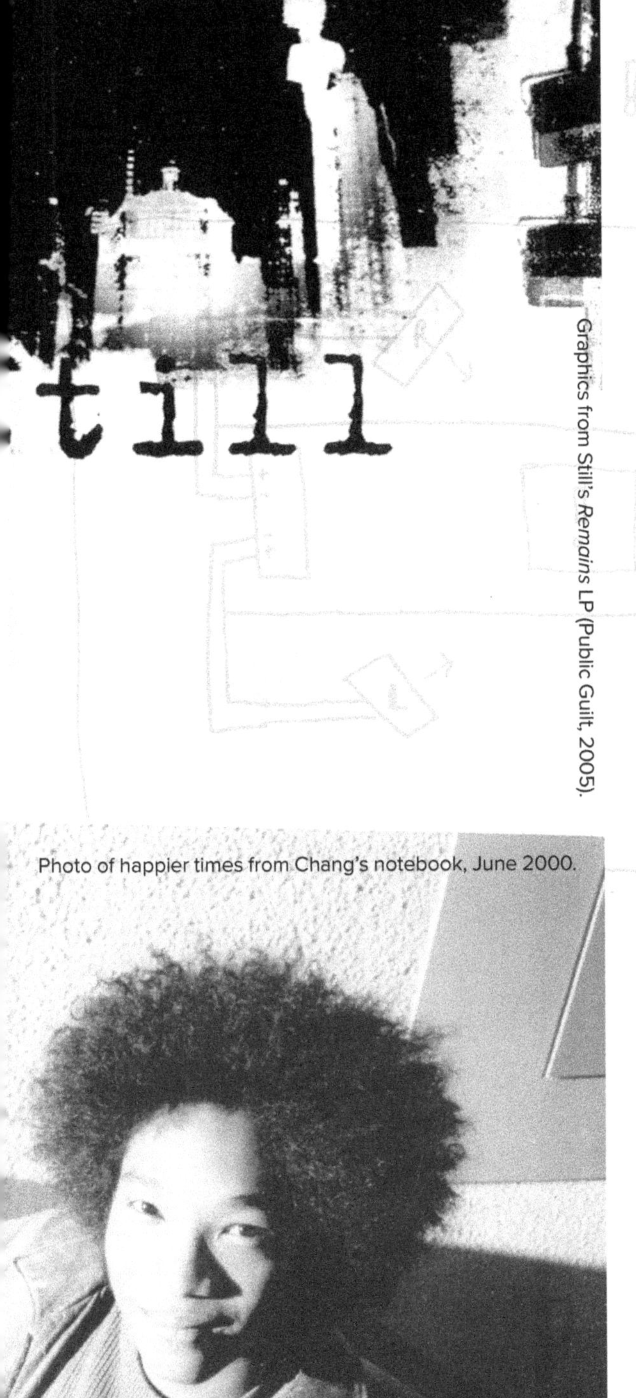

Graphics from Still's *Remains* LP (Public Guilt, 2005).

Photo of happier times from Chang's notebook, June 2000.

We had DJ Rek in the group since we started in '95, and he wasn't really into all the touring. We played a show at Swarthmore in 2001, and Chang was there helping us load in and set up. He knew of us and was a fan of our first album. He had bought it in Philly and was really into it. So that impressed us as at that point no one had really heard of us. Then when we finished sound-checking, Chang asked us if he could get on the turntables . . . He got on and blew us away! Rek was an amazing DJ who had come up in the old-school hip-hop era and eventually got more into DJing house and club music. He was incredible, but Chang was younger and coming out of the whole DMC scratch-battle DJ scene of that time. Guys like Qbert and Craze were his influences. Plus, he was really hungry and into it. At that point Rek had been touring with us for 5 years, and we could just tell he was over it. The thing that really sealed the deal was when the show was over, Chang helped us load all the gear out. Me and Will were like, 'I think we found our new DJ!'

⟶

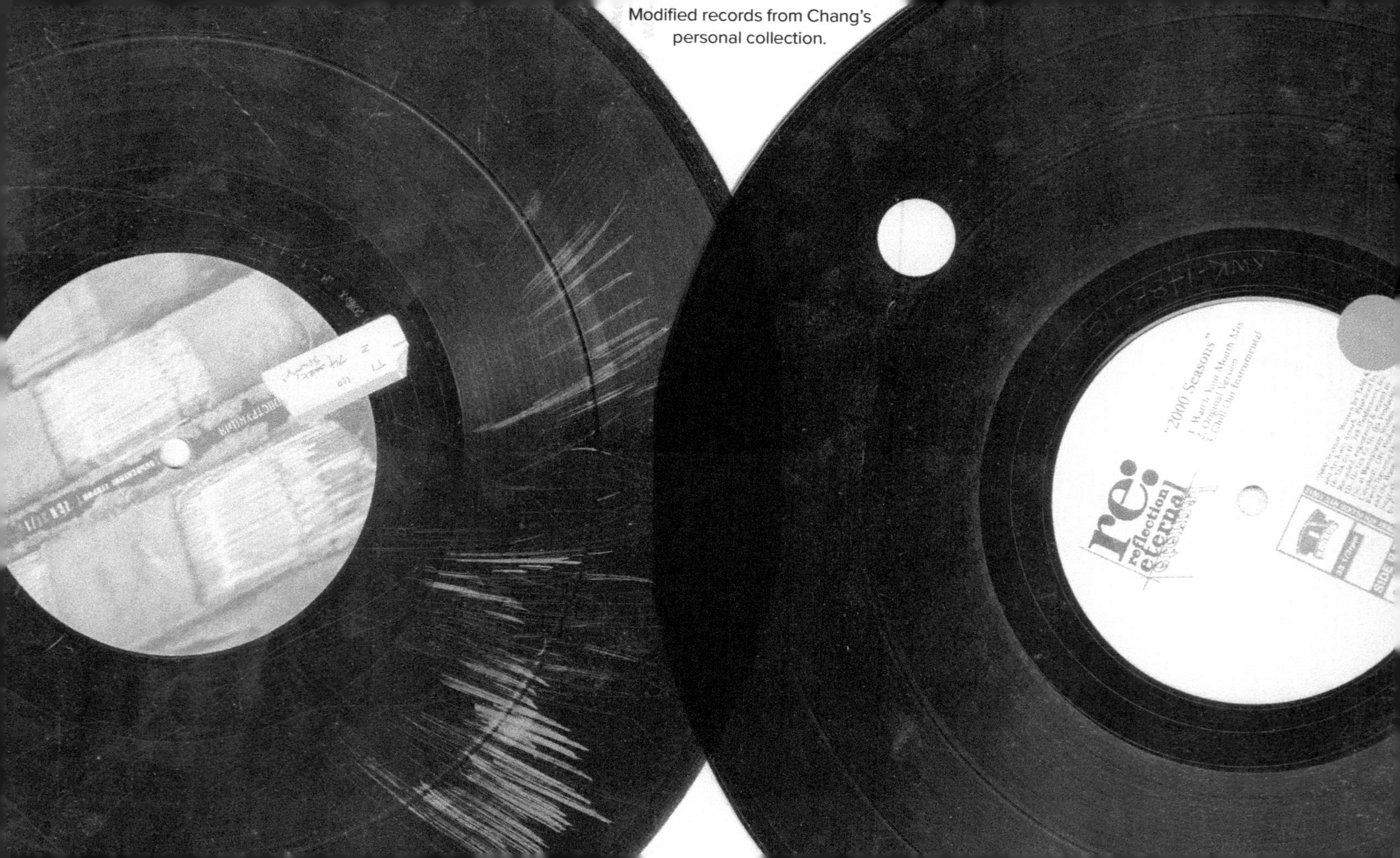
re:
reflection
eternal
"2000 Seasons"
1. Watch Your Mouth Mix
2. Original Version
3. Chill Out Instrumental
SIDE

Chang handled the turntables on dälek's *From Filthy Tongue of Gods and Griots* (Ipecac, 2002) and *Absence* (Ipecac, 2005), as well as their collaboration with krautrock legends Faust, *Derbe Respect, Alder* (Staubgold, 2004). "We spent years on the road in an era where ALL we did was tour," Will says. Those guys would all stay at my house whenever they came through.

I met Chang on stage. Alap and I had been corresponding via email leading up to a show in San Diego in 2002. During their set, I walked out behind them on stage to take some pictures, including the live shot here. "I wanted to kill you, man," Chang told me in my kitchen later that night. I guess they'd had security problems at the show the nights before in L.A. and San Francisco, so I was not exactly welcome to wander the stage that night.

During and after dälek, Chang was working on solo records and collaborations, each expanding his use of the turntable as an instrument and as a compositional tool. My favorite track is "Anodyne," the A-side from his Bomb Mitte 7" from 2002. It's a slow burn with a grating tension that finally erupts into a neck-flexing breakbeat. I used to drive late-night club-goers mad with it in my DJ sets.

Perhaps the most definitive musical statement Chang left us is the 6-track CD, *Remains* (Public Guilt, 2005). Don't get it distorted. What at first listen might sound unwieldy, chaotic, or barely planned-out is actually tightly controlled, intricately structured, and expertly executed. If nothing else, Chang was a composer. His sonic explorations were anything but random, and the sounds he used were carefully selected. Using unconventional source material and means to manipulate it, he built walls and wails and wound them together into compositions with peaks and bottoms and dynamics like any great song. The subtlety of the deep structures here are often lost in the noise on the surface. Listen to any of them at ample volume, and you'll hear it. Just play "Futility" or the live version of "Blindness." Their less-abrasive notes bely the noise of other tracks, revealing the nuance underneath.

Chang left us in 2018. Here's to his lasting legacy. ▲

Special thanks to Alap Momin, Will Brooks, Mike Manteca, and Erik Larson, and to Benjamin Tiven for additional materials.

Some of the artifacts from Chang's life in music were included in an exhibition at the Museum of Chinese in America, in NYC, which ran from May 2nd to September 29, 2019.

Diagrams and notes used in the backgrounds of these pages are from Chang's notebooks.

NOTES

1. Quoted in Ursula Block & Michael Glasmeier, *Broken Music: Artists' Recordworks.* Berlin, Germany: Berliner Kunstlerprogramm des DAAD, 1989, p. 73.

2. Public Enemy "Terminator X Speaks with His Hands" from *Yo! Bumrush the Show* [LP] Written by Chuck D, Flavor Flav, Eric Sadler, and Hank Shocklee. New York: Def Jam/Columbia, 1987.

3. Quoted in Dan Sperber, *Explaining Culture: A Naturalistic Approach*, New York: Blackwell, 1996.

michael cooper

BY SPIKE JONZE

i shot photographs of my friends riding and got paid for it. We all rode freestyle bikes, but they happened to be amazing at it. Brian Blyther, Ron Wilkerson, Matt Hoffman . . . and many others. The year was 1988 and the magazine was *Freestylin'*. Andy and Lew had hired me the previous year when I was 17 as an assistant editor. Then I started to get more into photography and eventually that's what I did. I would get to travel around with my friends who were

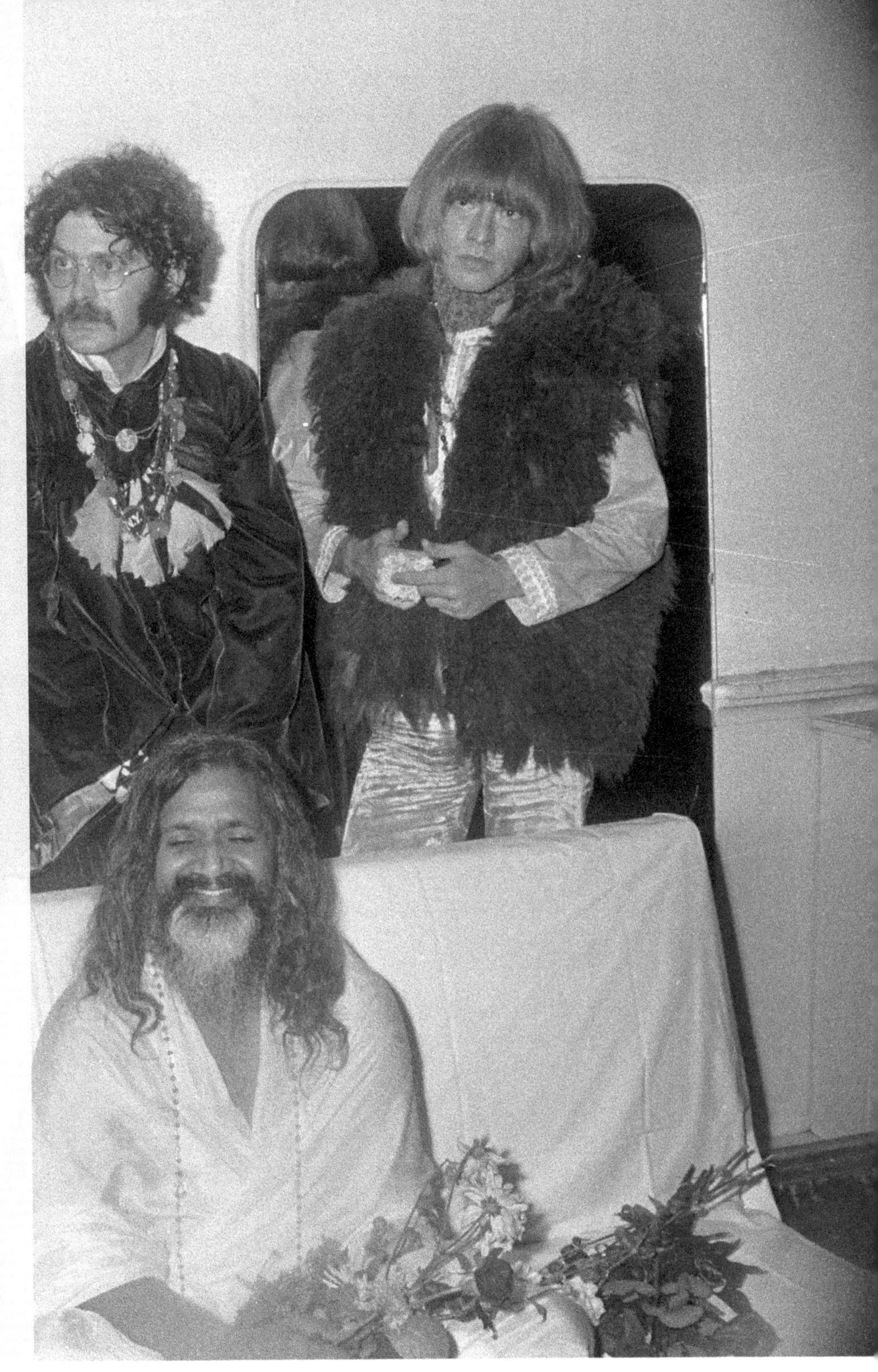

professional bike riders and take pictures of what
was around me. And these guys were amazing,
talented at pushing themselves to the limit. Twenty
feet above the ground, barely touching their bike, I
was awed and at the same time, part of their world.
There was nowhere else I wanted to be right then.

On a plane to another state, feeling young and
cocky, I was flipping through the airline magazine
and stumbled across an article about a guy from
the '60s who photographed the Rolling Stones and
the Beatles. The photographs that accompanied the
piece were all classic pictures of these rock and roll
legends. Some of the pictures are candid and some
are staged, but they are all the kind of photographs
that you can look at for a while and let your mind
wander across the images, drawing conclusions from
expressions and emotions from conclusions. The
article talked about how close he was with all these
guys and what a tight scene it was. He was friends
with the Stones before they were huge, when he was
my age, and he documented them as they exploded
in popularity to the point of packing stadiums.
  Reading about Michael Cooper, I instantly
related to him. His business and leisure were all
one. He was doing what he loved to do and that was
his life. I read on to discover he had also shot the
classic record covers of the Beatles' *Sgt. Pepper's* and
the Rolling Stones' *Their Satanic Majesties Request*.
He was doing such cool stuff, but what really hit
me was at the end of his story. When he was 31, he
killed himself. In a note he left, he explained by
saying something to the effect of the magic was
gone. He tasted so much and then stopped tasting.
  That's how I remember it at least, and as I read
those words, a wave of heat shot through my body.
I sat up straight, full of fear and—in a weird way—
inspiration.

I looked around the cabin of the plane. The other passengers were unaffected; they just kept on traveling, snoring, reading and chatting their way to their final destination. But it wasn't that easy for me. I'm not trying to be dramatic, but I was sincerely worried about what my final destination might be. I had a real fear that one day my wave of magic would fade away and all I'd be is an adult with a job. I couldn't bear the thought. I never felt suicidal or anything, but I couldn't imagine living a life that didn't awe and amuse me. How could it get better than this? Staying out all night with 15 guys, riding around downtown LA or flying to Mexico City with $18 and no ID, but knowing it all would work out, even if it meant selling unused film to tourists at the airport to get home.

So, when I read that this stranger from another world had similar feelings and didn't stick around to check it out, I thought I was doomed. I lived for years imagining I was approaching this impending page mark in my book of life, where instead of turning to the next page I would stop and flip back through the book, and find the best years of my life had happened ten chapters ago. I've come to learn that I'm not reading the book, but I'm writing it. Granted, I don't have complete creative control. There are many outside elements in my novel, but, if things ever cease being new and exciting, I do hold the pen.

What is it that makes you stop looking at things with wonder? How could Michael Cooper go from magic to misery? I hope I'll never know.

SPIKE JONZE is the versatile filmmaker behind the acclaimed films *Being John Malkovich*, *Adaptation*, and *her*. As a producer, his credits include Michel Gondry's *Human Nature* and Charlie Kaufman's *Synecdoche, New York*. He has directed numerous music videos, commercials, short films, and documentaries. He also serves as the creative director at VICE media and is one of the creators and producers of the *Jackass* TV show and films.

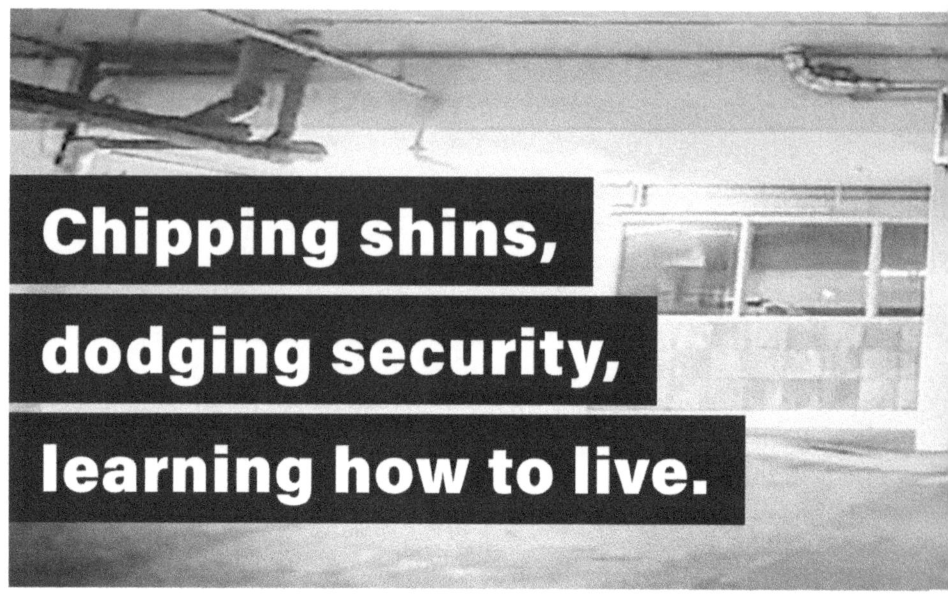

Chipping shins, dodging security, learning how to live.

I've spent much of my life in underground parking garages. I started when I was a pre-teen; today I'm 45, and the cold, unforgiving atmosphere of parking garages is like home to me.

The reason I hang out in parking garages is the same reason why when I run my fingers down my shins, I can feel countless indentations and chips in the bone; it's the same reason why I have fake bottoms on my top two front teeth; it's probably why my right elbow is messed up and sends unbelievable waves of pain through my body when I lean on it in just the right way.

The reason for all this is because I ride BMX flatland. I've ridden since I was 11, and I'll ride until I can't physically do it anymore. It's been a huge part of my life for longer than most things, and I've learned so much through the sport. And why parking garages? To ride flatland, especially at night, you need an indoor spot that's well-lit and flat and you can get away with riding in. That basically rules out everything except parking garages.

BMX flatland – for those not familiar with it, imagine doing breakdancing or figure skating on a BMX bike – is both an incredibly difficult and a solitary – and because of that, a very personal – sport. Although I have my riding crew, due to schedules – especially as we advance to this more vintage age – I find myself riding alone more and more. It is both incredibly peaceful – away from the chaos of my life with three kids and multiple jobs – and incredibly stressful – trying the same trick over and over and over again, down in the cold parking garage, unable to comprehend what exactly you're doing wrong. It's a finicky sport: maybe you need to lean half a degree

more – which feels like 30 degrees more – over your handlebars. Maybe you don't. Try, see what happens, fall to the ground, move on. It's the ultimate sport of trial and error. And error. And error. Then, the victory.

It's taught me the value of hard work more than any job ever has. I once worked on riding out of a single trick – the Smith decade – for two years. It took me two years to finally get my foot back on the pedal and ride away from that trick without touching the ground. It was completely psychotic: I was obsessed with the trick. I knew what I had to do – get my foot to land on the pedal – but I just couldn't make my foot do it. It was taking over my life. I'd go into the bathroom at work and mime doing the trick. I was having trouble focusing on my family life. I would try mental games – the ground is lava; I can have a special beer tonight if I pull it – and it didn't work. It just didn't click. Until it did.

Cut to a year later and two pretty bad wipeouts down in the parking garages doing that exact trick (one while riding alone, which is when riding alone starts to get pretty nerve-wracking): I stopped doing Smiths. I even took my brakes off my bike, so I couldn't do them if I wanted to (some riders do brakeless Smiths, but at my rate of progression, we're looking at a decade to learn that decade). Was all that work for nothing? No, because now I have my sights set on other tricks. Do it, and move on.

I was in the parking garages when I was just a kid, mind blown at what was possible on a bike. I was in them as a teenager, although (regrettably) less, as my bike took a backseat to other life pursuits. I was back in them in my 20s; I was

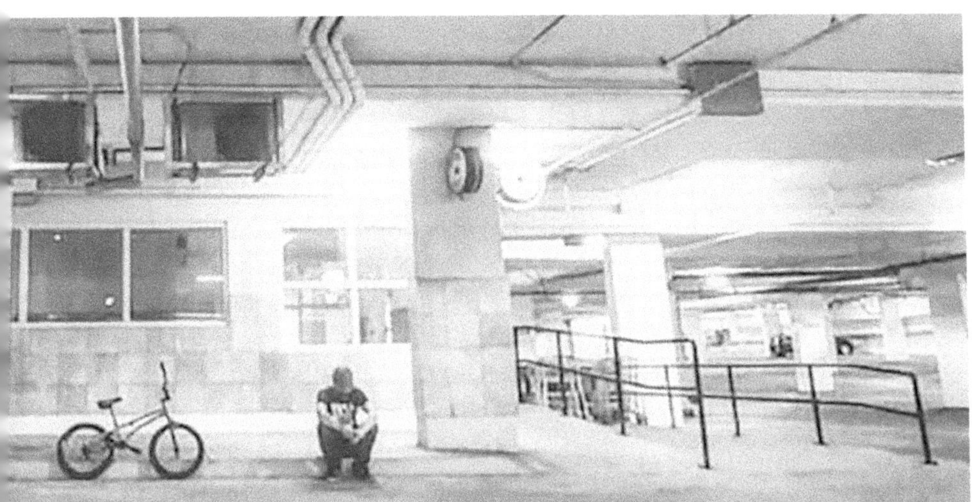

CONFESSIONS OF A FLATLAND BMX LIFER

in them even more in my 30s, after having my daughter, then my son. I remember being down in the parking garage the night Trump was elected. I was back in the parking garages in my early 40s, after my second son was born (not the night of; I'm not a complete heel). The parking garages are my home; the sound of my bike crashing to the ground, over and over and over, echoing off the walls, as I'm trying to learn a new trick is the most comforting sound in the world to me. I've fallen to parking garage floors so many times I can imagine how a parking garage floor feels right now, sitting here typing this. And it's relaxing to me to imagine that feeling.

Sometimes I sit and run my hand along my shins and feel the indents I've left there over the years. I think of hitting the concrete floor of parking garages at full speed on my chest without getting my hands out in time to protect me. I think of the countless, nameless faces of security guards telling me to move on. I think of the few who allowed me to stay, bless their hearts.

I'm a flatland rider. I'm 45 years old and have been riding since I was 11. I know that I'm racing the clock: I watch videos of my favorite pros – Benjamin Hudson, Dustyn Alt, Toon Pakphum – and think, That's what I want to be like. That's how good I will be. Then I take an honest look at my week's schedule, and I realize that, on one hand, it might be too late to ever get there.

But on the other hand, no fucking way. If spending countless – countless – hours alone on my bike down in the parking garage has taught me anything, it's that anything's possible. I've learned things on my bike I never thought I

would. I'm better now than I ever have been, easily, at 42. That's something 13-year-old me would never have believed. So, it's possible. It's cliché, but it's so true, and I really mean these words: Anything's possible.

But regardless of what the end result looks like – if I get Hudson-style flow or Pakphum-esque bangers, or if I never progress whatsoever past where I'm at today – I know at this point that I won't stop until the day my body hands in its two-week notice and tells me it can no longer live the parking-garage life. And when that day comes, I'll fight off the melancholy by looking back on all those hours spent in the cold parking garage, trying the same trick over and over and over, all those times I threw my bike or screamed out loud because I just couldn't get it, and I'll zoom in on the mental image to see the slight smile on my face. And I'll know it was all worth it.

This is the best sport in the world. It's taken so much out of me and put even more back in me. I can't imagine having lived a life without it.

GREG PRATT is a freelance writer for Decibel, bravewords.com, Outburn, and other publications. He's been riding BMX flatland for most his life but still has an incredible fear of his tires popping. He lives with his wife and three kids in Victoria, BC, Canada, where he calls parking garages "parkades."

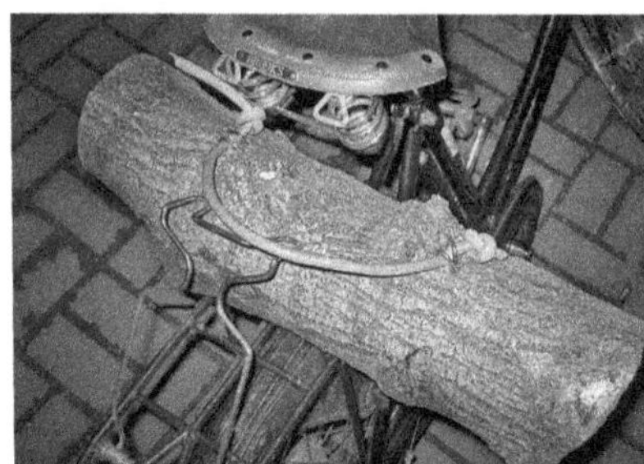

secret night-time bike club.

My friends were concerned about my bike ride home, I was not. The night had warmed up, no longer the 20 degrees the morning brought

I rode into my secret world.
With my bike.

Along the bike path, and up the hill.
Buchannan Street. Up the hill north of Columbia Pike.

I passed a sight beneath the streetlamp light.
Five perfect logs with straps stapled on like they were suitcases. I keep on going, with a stomach full of food and wine.
Wow... I must tell my friend Roni about that fantastic "trash pile" of logs with straps like little gifts to the world who might pass by.

Where am I? Yes... between South 6th and 5th on Buchannan.

Keep on going... up the hill. No... I must turn around. I must sacrifice the uphill for downhill, which is so hard to do. I have to witness the special passing gift.

Yes... they were what I saw. Five logs in a row with handles stapled on
I threw one on the back of my bike, so I have some kind of proof.
I rode back up the hill, in the opening where the trees separate and the light of the sky finds me, and there ahead was another bicyclist riding past.

We were alone at 10pm, riding in the dark and passing in the night. I waved, she, SHE said HI... and we knew we were part of the secret night-time bike club.

CYNTHIA CONNOLLY is a photographer, artist and curator from Washington, DC. She grew up in a community of musicians and artists who booked their own performances and produced and manufactured their own vinyl records. Recipient of two National Endowment for the Arts grants, she works for Arlington County, VA as a curator while wearing the tool belt of an artist. She continues to explore the world using art to create community, dialogue, and surprise in everyday life.

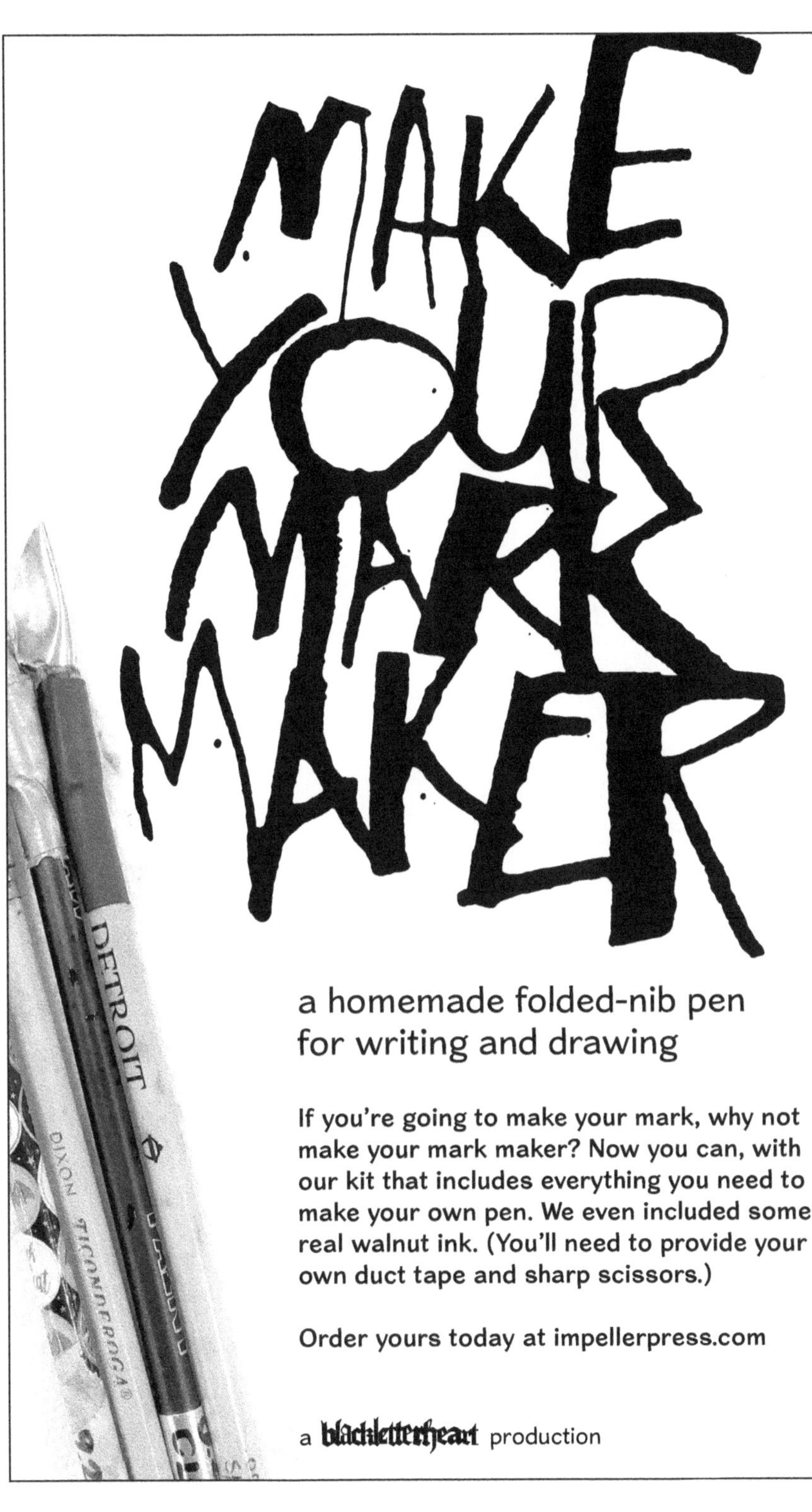

MAKE YOUR MARK MAKER

a homemade folded-nib pen
for writing and drawing

If you're going to make your mark, why not
make your mark maker? Now you can, with
our kit that includes everything you need to
make your own pen. We even included some
real walnut ink. (You'll need to provide your
own duct tape and sharp scissors.)

Order yours today at impellerpress.com

a blackletterheart production

DRAWIN

From day one you are moving on a line. A path leading forward from your present position. This line can be tracked whenever you look back into your past. This line is your history.

Do you ever wonder how many people have crossed over a certain spot on a sidewalk? One person creates a line, but that line has been repeated over and over again a million times. Yet each line is individual.

What if you walked to the same school for twelve years and one day you were suddenly able to retrace all of your past footsteps? Every path you walked for years to and from school— as though all your shoes had paint on their soles the whole time. You would see all the little variations you ever made on your walks. The different brands of shoes you wore. The different shoe sizes. But it would mostly be a dense pathway of black or whatever other color you imagined to be on the soles of your shoes. A diary of sorts.

Think about that occasionally... To be able to retrace all the lines you've made on a skateboard.

G LINES

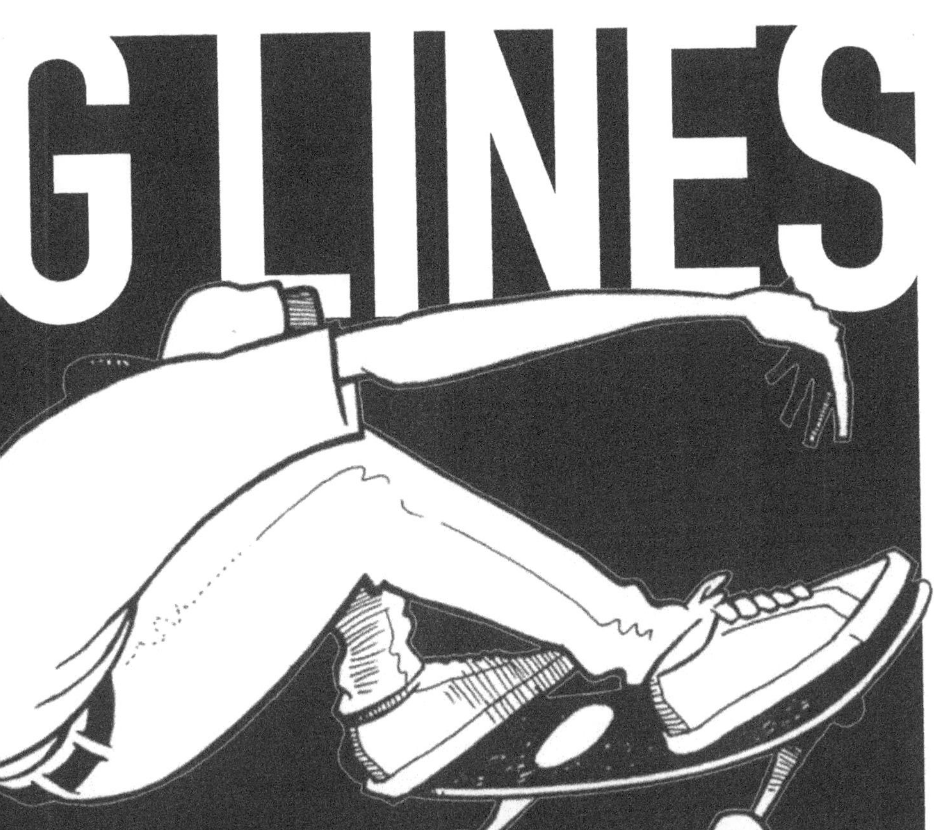

On a bike. In a car. On a bus. A plane. With a pen. Pencil. Chalk. In the sand. In your mind. A line can be something you draw mentally. A line can be physical... but several lines on a piece of paper can create the illusion of dimension. A line can hold order on a freeway. A clothesline. A line at the bank. A line is what you trace in your mind to reach a conclusion or solution. The right line can take you to a frontside grind in a pool or another to a ticket booth in a theater. Look behind to see old lines, then look forward to make up new ones.

ANDY JENKINS

is a multidisciplinary artist, artistic director, and creative conduit. He is the founder of Bend Press.

FISTS OF LOVE

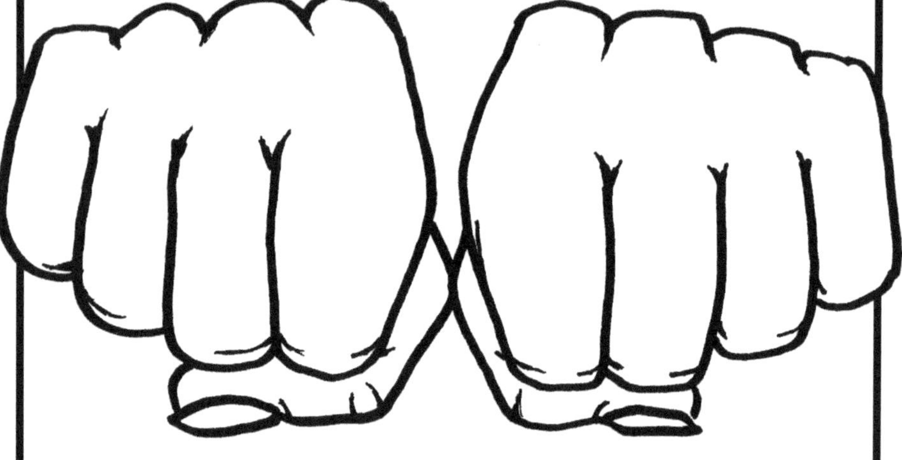

Fill in the knuckle tattoo above with the name
of your favorite eight-lettered artist!

A few of our suggestions:

KATE BUSH	IRMA BOOM	DAVID YOW	JOHN CAGE
PJ HARVEY	TOBI VAIL	PAUL RAND	TONY ALVA
BOB MOULD	BRUCE LEE	ANAIS NIN	ALICE BAG
PAT SMEAR	PAM GRIER	WILL SELF	DEL CLOSE
BRIAN ENO	MIKE WATT	SPIKE LEE	GEDDY LEE
GREG TATE	PHIL SHAO	TOM WAITS	MATT HART
MATT ROSS	KEN JEONG	TONY HAWK	BOBA FETT
MICA LEVI	CHIP KIDD	RYAN SHER	TED BUNDY
PAUL DANO	FRANK CHO	IRA LEVIN	LISA LOEB
TAE WON YU	GODFLESH	SHUN GREY	TOD SWANK
LIZ PHAIR	A$AP FERG	ELLE NASH	DEFTONES
NELS CLINE	DAME DASH	GREG SAGE	MARK DERY
JON BRION	JANE LEVY	DJ SHADOW	RICK ROSS
THRASHER	GARY HOLT	DAN KROHA	WILL WILES
OFWGKTA	JOHN MOHR	KIO STARK	MICK JONES
KIM DEAL	SAUL BASS	LINK WRAY	LILY RABE

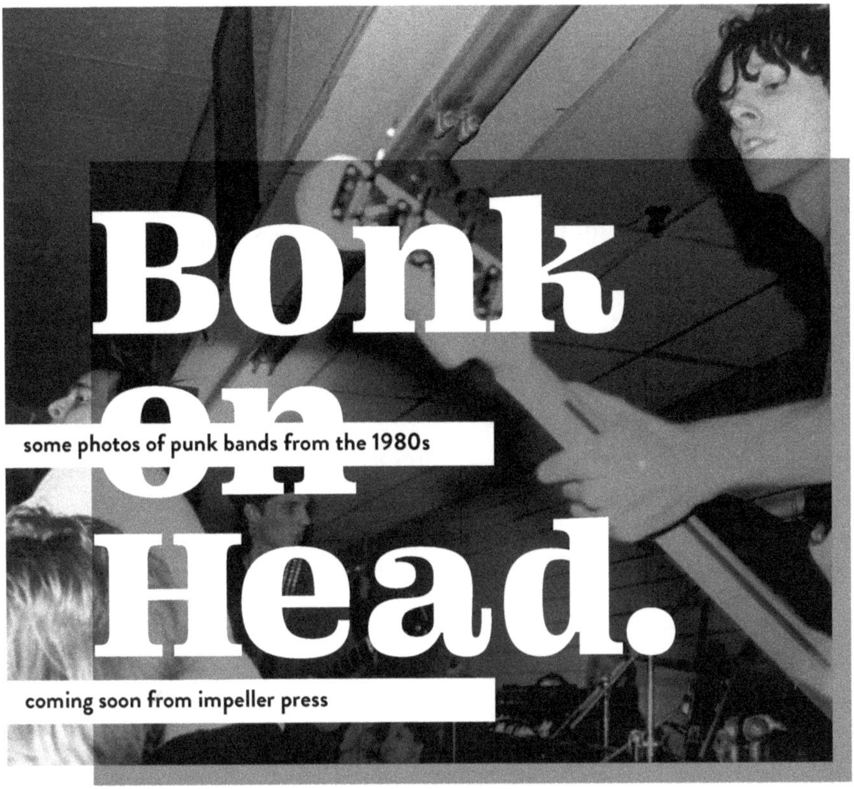

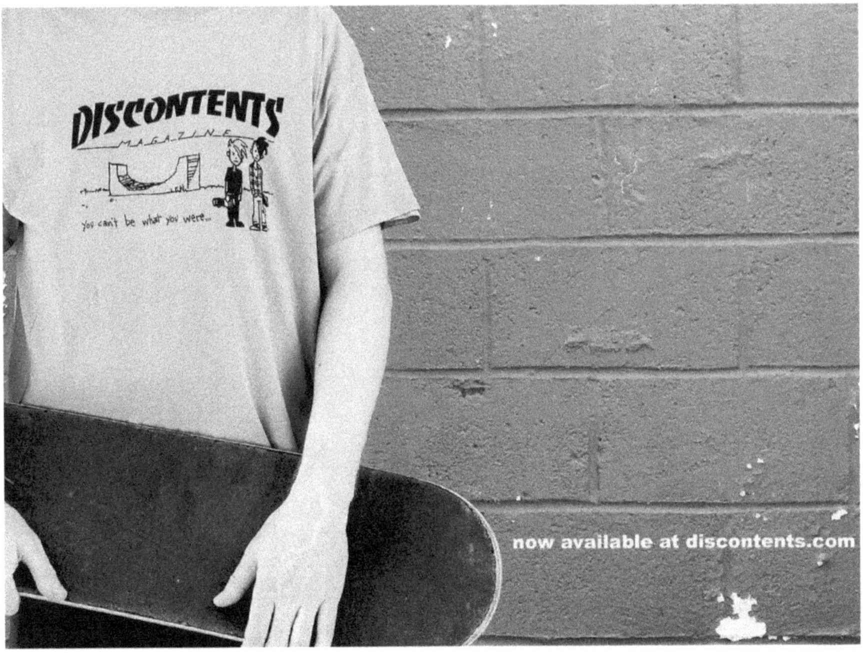

The Livest One Peter Relic

Don the Engineer moves to wrap
a swath of sheer, pantyhose-like fabric around the Shure 122
microphone, to keep sibilant sounds from popping on tape,
as well as spittle and slobber away
But Biggie's already ready, going in, rapping
Live from Bedford Stuyvesant, the livest one . . .
and if spit can be immortal, well
You knew he was special,
this fat fuck in the fruity Coogi sweater besmirched with burger grease,
that he'd change the way rhymes rhyme
and the type of tales the tellers told
and so, dissolving, you took an Alka-Seltzer and lay down.

When you awoke
from this shock nap, 60/40 sure
you'd been dreaming, Biggie was still on the mic:
Fuck the state pen, I fuck hoes at Penn State . . .
Biggie, you say,
my niece Jesse goes to Penn State
can't you change
it to Boise State, or Alcorn State
or Norm Van Brocklin Community College?
and damn if you didn't feel like taking
another Alka- and a couple Bromo-Seltzers
chugging a whole bottla pussy pink Pepto
and toking a bolster-thick blunt besides
but all there is is
a broken folding chair
and a crenelated quart of Crown Royal
as empty as a live bait bucket
that Big drunk all of,
all by hisself.

Biggie laughs
an incense-drenched, blunt-occluded chuckle,
like carbon exhaust from a Stealth bomber, as if to say
you ain't listening . . . you don't hear me doe
but aye, you are listening
it's just you can't hardly heed what you're hearing
a black fact
which hasn't changed
all these years
after the assassination
and the quickie biopic
and the host of pretenders
barnaclinging to the throne.

Shit is this what he meant by life after death
after the last breath
a lasting last laugh,
heh-heh.

Trick Bag

Peter Relic

The black kid
in the black cap
that says
MAKE HARDCORE MELODIC AGAIN
has a point.

Many points,
flinty points,
glinty points,
spiky studs
of corrosive chrome
gracing the back
of his black denim vest
with its switchblade-sliced sleeves,
puckered piky purposeful
points spelling out
BEATNIGS.

This crumbling curb
beside a red railing
isn't his
but it is: his
claim as great
as anyone who ever shredded
a painted lane
and rolled away
close to clean.

Which is when the man
whose slacks are as white
as his fat pink face
approaches his fat ass Porsche,
juggling beeping key fobs,
Siamese iPhones
and a 64-ounce cup
of something disgusting.

He glares.
He stares.
He steps toward the kid
now sitting cigarette-less
on the skate-scarred railing.

Nosebone
feeble grind
to hard flip!
he says.
Hardcore!

They smack
palms twice
then backs of hands,
stacking fist bumps to squid fingers.

Yeah right!

The man huffle-slumps into his shiny sedan,
revving its engine with gusto.

The kid gets up grinning,
aiming his board again
down the lane.

PETER RELIC is the author of *Ping Pong On The Periodic Table* (Bat One Thousand Books). He lives in Savannah, Georgia.

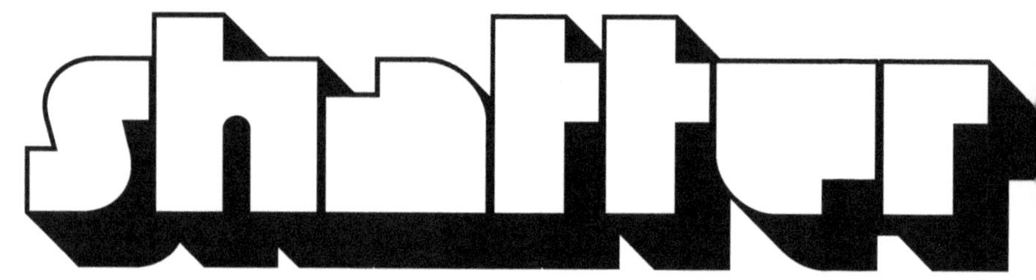

AN INTERVIEW WITH

James Ward Byrkit

WE'VE ALL BEEN AT A DINNER PARTY where the dynamic seemed to sour as the night progressed. What if the dynamic not only went bad but splintered into multiple realities? James Ward Byrkit's 2013 film, *Coherence*, is just such a gathering.

Coherence is the product of pulling back. After working on big-budget movies (e.g., *Rango*, the *Pirates of the Caribbean* series, etc.), Byrkit wanted to strip the process down to as few pieces as possible. Instead of a traditional screenplay, he spent a year writing a 12-page treatment. Filmed over five nights in his own house, *Coherence* documents a dinner party gone astray as a comet flies by setting off all sorts of quantum weirdness. The story is small enough to tell among friends over dinner but big enough to disrupt their beliefs about reality. With the dialog unscripted, the film unfolds like a game. Each actor was fed notecards with short paragraphs about their character's moves and motivations. Like a version of *Clue* written by Erwin Schrödinger, *Coherence* works because of its limited initial conditions, not in spite of them.

Byrkit's latest project is an anthology of episodes in what sounds like the aftermath of the events in *Coherence*. The series is called *Shatter Belt*, and Byrkit is currently filming and raising money for it simultaneously.

ROY CHRISTOPHER So, *Shatter Belt* picks up where *Coherence* left off, right? The reality-splintering event happened in *Coherence* and *Shatter Belt* follows the aftermath.

JAMES WARD BYRKIT So, *Shatter Belt* is not the sequel to *Coherence*, but it's definitely a follow-up, meaning we're using much of the same process and philosophy and thematic elements and actors of that film. *Shatter Belt* is a collection of short stories that involve consciousness and the nature of reality, each episode a self-contained story a la *Twilight Zone*. Like *Coherence*, the ideas are immediate and pure, unfiltered by studio executives or the Hollywood process. These are micro-budget productions of giant concepts. Like *Coherence*, there

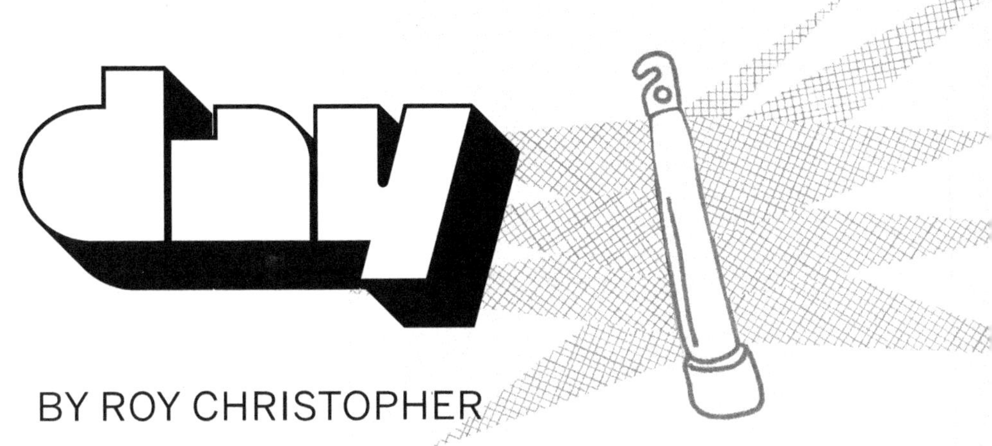

BY ROY CHRISTOPHER

is almost no crew of any kind. No art department, no costume department. No special effects. The actors have to be on their A game to even get through a day because of the flexibility required.

After years of trying to get smart challenging sci-fi projects greenlit the old-fashioned way, it became clear that again, my only option was going to be just picking up a camera and to start shooting. No permission needed.

RC Weirdly, it seems that in making both *Coherence* and *Shatter Belt* you've had to grapple with the same problems that an Everett many-worlds interpretation of quantum realities presents. I know you spent a year plotting out the possibilities of *Coherence*, but how do you keep these stories from spinning off into complete chaos?

JWB This is a question that might be better saved when we really do roll out a *Coherence* sequel, which has been in the works for a year. And yes, that's often the main focus, keeping the stories relevant and connected even as the chaos creeps in. I find weeks of letting the stories play out organically in my head during long walks will slowly reveal an overall shape and recurring ideas that can then be the beginning of a structure.

[WARNING: SPOILER BELOW]

RC How important is the *whisper* of ketamine to the plot of *Coherence*?

JWB Ha! The *whisper* is what makes the concoction dangerous/mysterious/potent/magical/useful. But she had to say it that way to make it sound like it was also safe and recreational. We wanted the ketamine to serve double duty—ONE: to provide a possible explanation of the strange communal meltdown that was occurring at the party... (and pulling everyone into the kitchen so that Hugh and Amir could be alone in the living room and escape with the box) and TWO: as a way for EM to knock herself out without killing herself. ∎

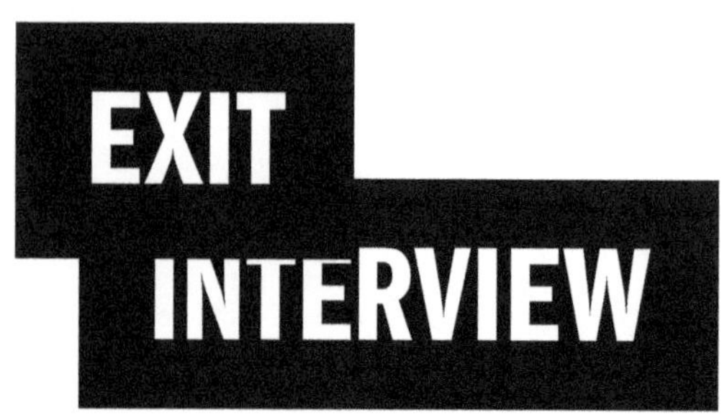

Marnie Ellen Hertzler

BY ROY CHRISTOPHER

A small band of rapping misfits convened in a wasteland commune, weed-bent on making music for their masses and a self-sustainable community for themselves. Sadboy, Keem, Mijo, RyBundy, Huckleberry, Phong Winna, Benz Rowm (RIP), and Champloo Sloppy set up camp in the desert near Crestone, Colorado. Having gone to high school with most of these guys, Marnie Ellen Hertzler went to document. The result is the 2020 documentary film, Crestone, *a delirious detour through the chaos and contradictions of coming of age in a future that's already ending.*

Hertzler is currently in production on her second feature, called Eternity One, *about a disappearing island community.*

How much of *Crestone* was planned beforehand?

Much of it was planned. We only had 8 days to shoot so I wanted to be sure I had some kind of structure for those 8 days so they wouldn't slip away. The guys and I had scripted some scenes together and I had roughed out a narrative through-line. The best parts in the film just happened on their own. It is nice to be able to work so freely that, when needed, you can bring the happenstance to the front. Documentary isn't real, and Narrative isn't fake. I wanted to lean into that notion and planned to do so.

Did you plan to be a part of the film?

I forget if I had planned to be a part of the film. Probably. It seems so long ago now. For many of the early cuts I wasn't in it at all. Those cuts were nice, but they weren't the film I wanted to make. So much of the film is about the experience of making it, so putting me in there was necessary to communicate that.

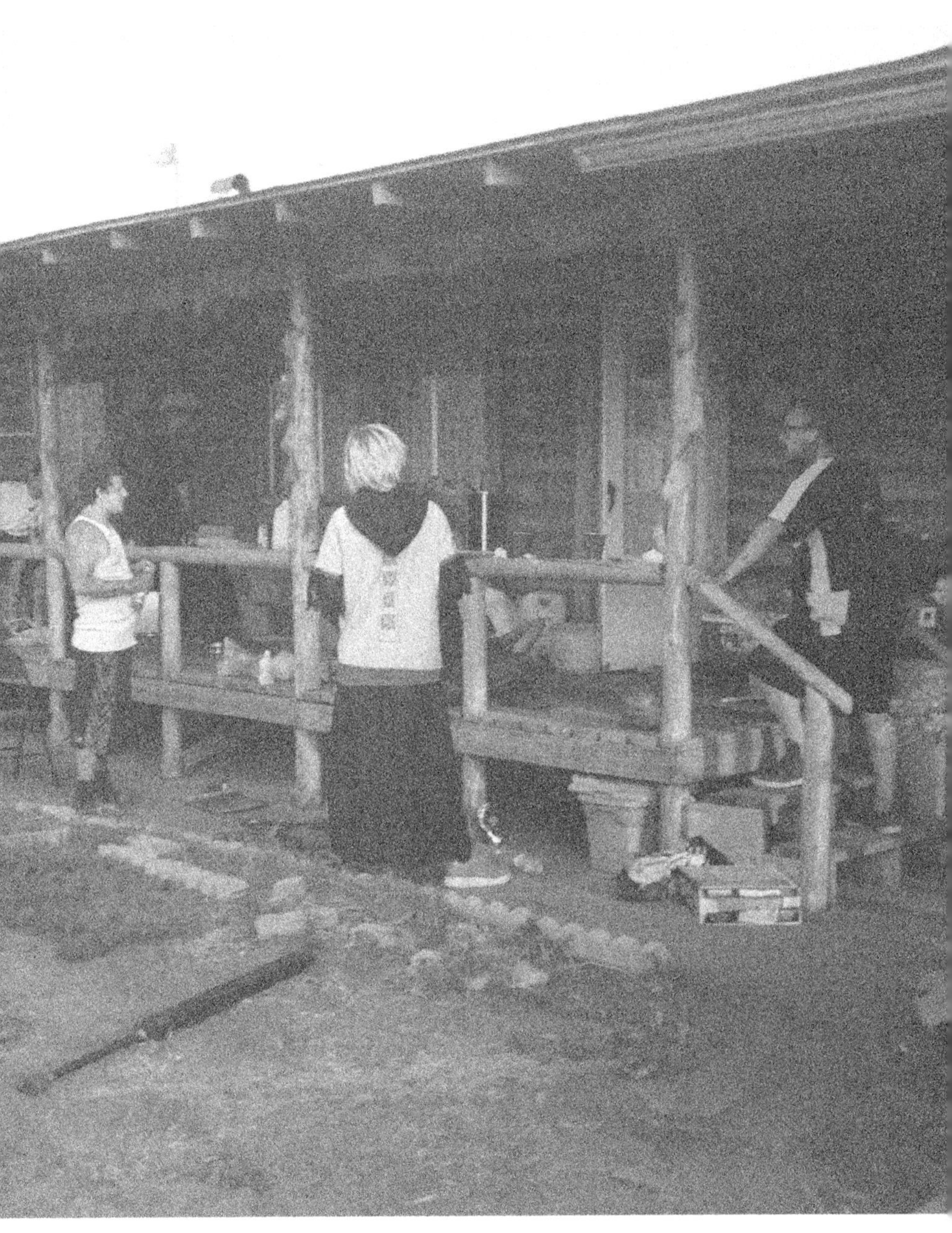

Champloo Shloppy, Huckleberry, and Benz Rowm talking shop.
Photo by Marnie Ellen Hertzler.

Did the movie turn out anything like you were expecting?

No. But to be fair, I had no expectations at all, and I worked hard to maintain the zero expectations. I did know we would at least come home with a couple of music videos and maybe a short. But somehow, we were able to dig out a feature film.

The juxtaposition of high-desert communal brotherhood with Soundcloud raps is compelling but also haunting. There are moments in the film when it really does feel like the world is ending. Did it feel that way out there?

The world was ending, in a way. It always feels like the world is ending to me wherever I go. But, yes, in Crestone in particular. The desert is terrifying and electric. Everything is loud, silent, large, miniscule all at the same time. When you go to sleep at night it feels like you never know what you will wake up to the next morning. But also, we build worlds within our relationships and the love we create with other people. Those worlds are so tenuous and delicate.

Who was that one dude who just showed up out there?

The guy chopping wood? That's Huckleberry. He's a gem. I love that guy. He has the worst jokes, best laugh, and a very buttery southern accent. He's a very talented model. He was living in Denver at the time and had become friends with some of the guys. He heard we were shooting a movie. Sadboy showed me his Instagram while we were prepping to come out there and I obviously wanted to meet him. Lucky for me, he decided to show up.

What's next for you?

I'm working on a new feature film now about Transhumanism and the Chesapeake Bay, exploring the many ways we seek salvation. ■

Marnie Ellen Hertzler capturing the calm in the chaos.

not necessarily GOSPEL

a comic by Roy Christopher

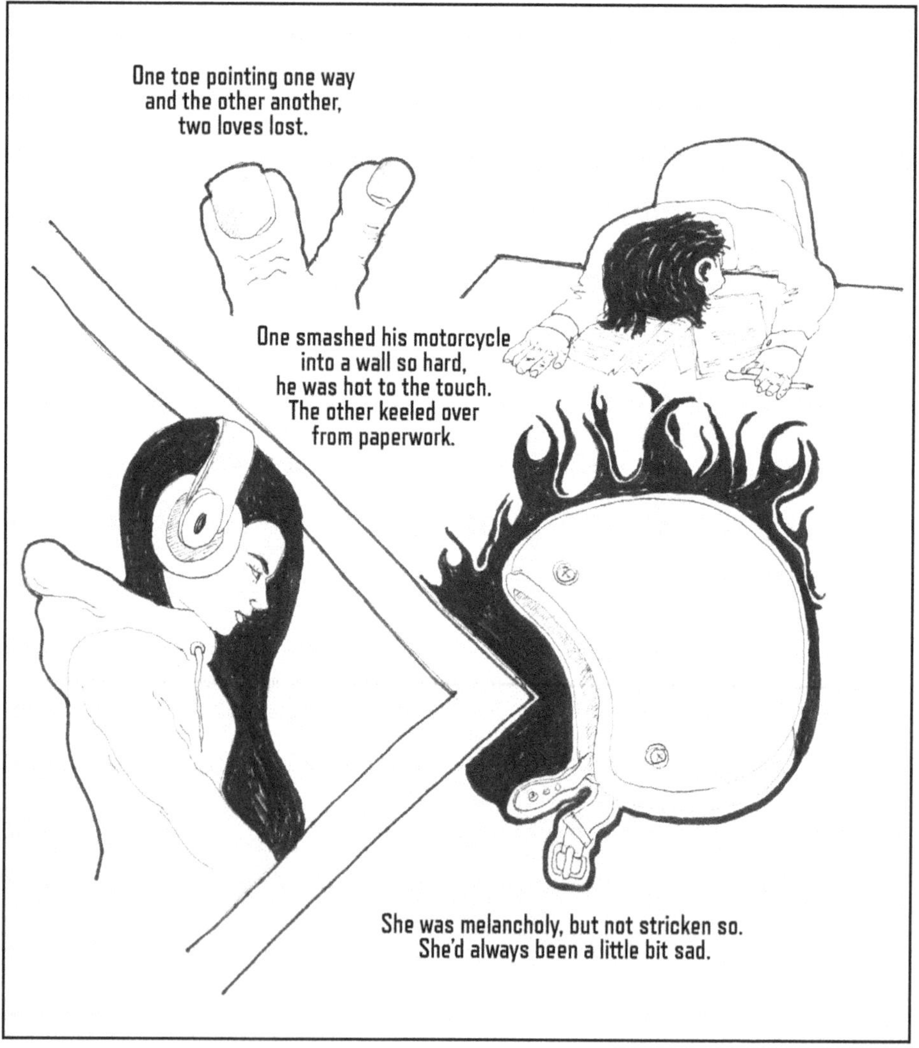